The Potty Journey

Guide to Toilet Training Children with Special Needs, Including Autism and Related Disorders

Judith A. Coucouvanis

APC

Autism Asperger Publishing Company
P.O. Box 23173
Shawnee Mission, Kansas 66283-0173
877-277-8254 • www.asperger.net

APC

©2008 Autism Asperger Publishing Company
P.O. Box 23173
Shawnee Mission, Kansas 66283-0173
877-277-8254 • www.asperger.net

Publisher's Cataloging-in-Publication

Coucouvanis, Judith A.
   The potty journey : guide to toilet training children with special needs, including autism and related disorders / Judith A. Coucouvanis. -- 1st ed. -- Shawnee Mission, Kan.: Autism Asperger Pub. Co., 2008.

      p. ; cm.
      ISBN: 978-1-934575-16-1
      LCCN: 2007939601
      Includes bibliographical references.
      Summary: Systematic, comprehensive and proven way to toilet train children with autism and related disorders, whose very characteristics make toilet training challenging. The author takes a humorous approach to an otherwise difficult task.

      1. Toilet training. 2. Children with disabilities--Education. 3. Children with disabilities--Care. 4. Parents of autistic children--Handbooks, manuals, etc. 5. Parents of children with disabilities--Handbooks, manuals, etc.
   I. Title. II. Guide to toilet training children with special needs, including autism and related disorders.

HQ770.5 .C68 2008
649.62--dc22   0712

This book is designed in Frutiger and Bermuda.

Printed in the United States of America.

*To the families who invited me
to come with them on
their potty journeys –
with much respect and admiration.*

FOREWORD

I met Judy Coucouvanis when my son, Alex, was 4 years old. In spite of his complicated learning challenges, Alex was a happy, clever boy – with a very willful temperament. It seemed to me that he had the intellectual and psychological readiness to be potty trained from the age of 3, but he resisted all of my well-thought-out efforts. After a year of trying without success, we finally met Judy, and Alex was completely potty-trained within about six weeks.

Judy's strategies went beyond the typical methods I had been trying, but were gentle and respectful. She helped me understand how to motivate Alex to cooperate by using his special interests and positive reinforcements. This information was invaluable, not only because Alex was successful potty-trained, but because it gave me an understanding of Alex's unique thought processes. Judy's methods enabled me to feel more confident and capable of helping my "strong-minded" child to learn new skills and develop healthy, appropriate behavior.

To parents of children with special needs, please know that the immense grief and frustration you may be feeling right now can be overcome when you have the right information and are willing to put forth consistent efforts. This is very critical. The job is difficult, but the rewards are well worth it. I am proud to say that Alex is a beautiful, well-behaved teenager, and I am truly grateful to Judy for all that she has done to help us through the years. Exceptional people like Judy really know how to show us the way. Listen. It works.

Bonnie McDonald

TABLE OF CONTENTS

INTRODUCTION
A Word to the Tour Director

The *Potty Journey* is a systematic and comprehensive toilet training guidebook. It is not a book of "toileting tricks." Step-by-step, it leads you, the tour director, all the way through the toilet training journey to its ultimate destination: successfully toilet training your child with special needs. Whether you have tried potty training in the past and given up or have never tried, this book is for you. The trip is plotted in detail and includes a comprehensive itinerary for the entire toileting journey. You will learn about extensive, yet simple-to-do data collection, how to use rewards, the importance of routine, the impact of a consistent schedule, and the significance of dry pants.

This book is about success, removing the barriers that can affect toilet training and embracing the child's abilities in order to find the solutions that will help achieve continence. So plan to set aside time to read and study this book.

Give this job the same value as other worthwhile activities in your life. After all, you don't need me to tell you how important the successful conclusion of this journey is to your child's future. His social acceptance by peers, school placement decisions, and eventual job opportunities depend upon it.

You are about to embark on an exciting expedition. Many others have successfully traveled this road before you, as illustrated in the following excerpts.

As the Pediatric Rehab Social Worker at William Beaumont Hospital in Royal Oak, I am always attempting to identify resources to meet the many needs of our parents who have children with special needs.

On a consistent basis I am asked for information/resources regarding toilet training special needs children. Since 2002 Judy Coucouvanis has come to our department and presented her material in a workshop format.

Parents tell other parents about her presentation. It is the best form of validation when I hear from a parent that another parent has been successful with toileting. The word of mouth about her process spreads throughout our waiting rooms. Parents have told me her presentation was the best no-nonsense approach they have ever tried.

– Therese T. Scarpace, LMSW

I am a physical therapist who works in the school setting with students ages 3-26. For the past three years, I have used and instructed parents to use the method of toilet training Judy Coucouvanis outlines in *The Potty Journey*. The students and families I've assisted have achieved incredible success. The program is easy to understand and, more important, easy to implement. Families have seen life-changing results in a very short period of time. Thank you, Judy!!!

– Cheryl Guy, PT, Rochester Community Schools, Rochester, Michigan

Bon Voyage!

CHAPTER 1
THE POTTY TRAVELERS:
Children with Special Needs

All children are unique. Some are energetic, distractible, or impulsive. Others are quiet and withdrawn. Some are funny, while others are serious. Some have language skills, and some do not. Some have cognitive, sensory, physical or mobility limitations. Some have fears and anxieties, while others have no fears whatsoever. Some children have special needs, while others have special talents. Each child has her own individual personality and set of personal characteristics that will influence all aspects of life, including the toileting journey.

Children with Autism Spectrum Disorders

When your child has an autism spectrum disorder or a related disorder, the toileting journey can be especially challenging. Those adults who do not fully understand the child with autism often perceive his unique characteristics as an overwhelming barrier to successful toileting. However, when you understand how to address these characteristics, the likelihood of successful continence increases immensely.

The specific characteristics of autism that can affect toilet training include the following:
- need for routine and sameness
- communication
- social interaction/learning
- sensory stimulation
- learning profile
- biological functions

Let's briefly look at each of these areas.

Need for Routine

The child who has a strong need for routine will likely resist your request to sit on the potty as well as your expectation that he begin to eliminate in the toilet. After all, he has probably been eliminating in a diaper for many years. Now you are asking him to do something new and different.

Changing a routine for a child with autism or a related disorder can be very difficult and often must be done slowly. Chapter 6: *Avoiding Disaster* instructs you in how to introduce the new expectation that your child sit on the toilet and how to teach him to stay there for longer periods of time.

Communication

If your child has communication deficits (most children with an autism spectrum disorder do), she might not understand the words you use to explain your new expectations. She may not even comprehend what you are asking her to do.

Be very clear in your communication and use pictures, symbols, or even objects, in addition to your words. Some parents expect a child to tell them when he needs to use the bathroom. This is often unrealistic in the early stages of potty training. Temporarily, let go of the belief that your child will come and get you, or notify you in some other way when she needs to use the toilet. We talk more about this in Chapter 12: *Creating Independent Travelers*.

Social Interaction/Learning

Typically, children with autism do not respond favorably to achieving social status, such as becoming a "big boy" or a "big girl" – terms that are often used to motivate young children. These abstract concepts have little meaning for the child who is often very concrete in his thinking. In fact, this child may think sitting on the potty will help him to grow in size (become "bigger").

Another challenge can occur if your child does not like social interaction, or places little to no importance upon pleasing you. Such children often prefer to be alone. Your child might not respond to your use of praise, hugs and smiles as a reward for going to the bathroom. As a result, you might become frustrated trying to find a powerful social motivator or reinforcer.

Brainstorming ideas with friends, family members, and your child's school team can generate a list of possibilities. Using reinforcers is discussed in Chapter 4: *Travelers' Compensation: Using Rewards.*

Sensory Stimulation

Some children with autism have difficulty with sensory information. They may not be able to "feel" the need to eliminate as they cannot read their body's signals to urinate or defecate. Some hold their urine or bowel movements for hours or even days, while others eliminate seemingly at random intervals. A few children enjoy the feel of feces and "paint" it on walls and furniture. Such occurrences are exasperating for everyone involved and require creative solutions. Some children are sensitive to sounds and may not like the sound of the flushing toilet. Others who are sensitive to touch may rebel at the feel of a cold toilet seat, rough toilet paper, or paper towels.

Recognizing and understanding your child's sensitivities will help you decide how to proceed on the journey. Suggestions for dealing with sensory concerns are located throughout the book, but especially in Chapters 9 and 10, where accidents, mishaps and obstacles are discussed.

Learning Profile
Often children with autism have associated learning problems. For example, it frequently takes them much longer to learn a new skill than typical peers. Toileting is no exception. Also, they may be easily distracted, frustrated, cry, whine, or even tantrum.

Using effective teaching strategies and patience will be your staunchest ally. Pay close attention to how to use rewards as detailed in *Chapter 4: Travelers' Compensation* and how to use visual supports described in *Chapter 7: Final Preparations*.

Biological Functions
Finally, it is not uncommon for children with autism to demonstrate irregular patterns of urination and/or defecation due to biological reasons. For example, some

children eat very restricted diets, while others have food sensitivities. Some have problems with chronic constipation, and others have very loose stools.

These issues can make toilet training a special challenge and are addressed in Chapter 10: *Other Bowel Training Obstacles and Predicaments.*

The Good News!!

Despite obstacles and special considerations, toilet training your child with special needs is achievable. Countless children with varied abilities are successfully using the toilet independently and semi-independently. *The Potty Journey* is a program to help your child be successful in this area. Toilet training does not usually happen spontaneously. Like many other skills, toileting requires systematic methods and guided practice.

Now that you know the challenges you face, let's talk briefly about toileting and typically developing children in order to learn about the skills that are part of the toileting sequence.

The Typical Journey

Research conducted by Schum et al. (2002) describes the sequence of toilet training skills and the age at which typically developing American children attain these skills. This range of skills helps to define what is "normal."

For those of us who are working or living with a child with special needs, there is no easily determined "typical" or "normal" sequence. A child may be able to pull pants up or down but not show interest in using the potty. A child may stay dry throughout the night but refuse to sit on the toilet in the morning. Children may not understand "potty words" or be able to tell during or after having a bowel movement (BM) because they have no language.

Nevertheless, in my experience, information about typically developing children can reveal the relevant skills for your child with special needs. For this reason, I have included the tasks described by Schum et al. (2002) in Appendix A, *Toilet Training: The Journey.* It is a useful tool for assessing your child's current progress and determining what applicable skills she might also need to learn. To use the tool, simply indicate what your child can do at the start of the journey, at mid-point and at the end. Once the child has accomplished all of the pertinent skills, celebrate with a party, because you have reached your final destination.

Toilet Training Dos and Don'ts

Few other skill deficits bring out such a range of emotions in caregivers as potty training. Common emotions include disappointment, guilt, anger, frustration, and hopelessness. Here are a few words to the wise:

1. Remain calm while the child is sitting on the toilet and when the child has an accident.

2. Avoid blame, shame, and threats. These actions do not encourage the child to try to learn what you are asking him to do.

3. Strive to remain matter-of-fact and encourage the child to try to stay dry. Don't act upset, scold, or punish the child who has an accident.

4. Be positive and encouraging. Praise the child's efforts and when she is successful.

5. Don't feel pressured by well-meaning family members and friends.

6. Don't give up; get help – more about this later.

I am a mother of twin boys born premature. They were delayed in every aspect of their lives (speech, motor skills, etc.). I had tried potty training them in the "traditional" way with no success. The boys were 4-1/2 years old and I didn't see them ever being potty trained. That's when I attended a seminar given by Judith Coucouvanis. After listening to her techniques, I went home and completely revamped the way that I was assisting my boys in their "training." It was a lot of work (I am not sure anything is easy with special needs children!), but finally we had success!!!! I owe it all to Ms. Coucouvanis and her great techniques.

– Karen Lorenz, mother of twin boys

CHAPTER 2
SIGNS AND SIGNALS
on the Potty Journey

Sometimes it is difficult to know when to start the toilet training journey. You may be waiting for your child to show interest in using the potty. However, my experience has been that many children with special needs usually do not show such an interest. In fact, they often have no clue that the potty is for their use, too. Therefore, part of your job as potty tour director will be to teach them what the toilet is used for.

Signs of Readiness

Some parents believe they should wait for the child to somehow indicate that she is wet or soiled, perhaps by bringing a clean diaper or removing a wet or soiled one. Again, it is common for a child with special needs not to do this. However, some children may indicate they are wet or soiled, and this is one of the signs that a child is ready for the potty journey. The other signal of readiness is that the child stays dry through the night. If your child exhibits either of these signs, you can be reassured that your child is "ready" to begin.

Two Absolute Signs of Readiness

1. Your child indicates when his diaper is wet or soiled or in some way "asks" to be changed. Perhaps he brings a clean diaper to you, removes a soiled diaper or, in some cases, even changes his own diaper.

2. Your child usually remains dry through the night.

If the child does not exhibit these signs, she is ready if she meets the following guidelines.

When to Start the Potty Journey

While parents of typically developing children are told by professionals to begin potty training when the child is between 2 and 3 years of age, parents of special needs children are often told to "wait and see." Sometimes this is sound advice, but it can perpetuate wetting and soiling. This is particularly true for children with autism spectrum disorders. These children learn by routine. Once a fixed routine is established (such as urinating and defecating in diapers or pull-ups), the more difficult it becomes to change that routine and adjust to the new routine of using the toilet. Therefore, it is often prudent to begin toilet training if the following guidelines are met.

Child Remains Dry for 1-2 Hours

The ability to hold urine is a sign of physiological readiness and an indicator that the child is physically able to temporarily store body wastes in order to stay dry and clean. If the child is unable to stay dry for 1-2 hours, and is 4 years or older, she should be referred to a health professional to check for kidney, urinary tract, or bladder abnormalities. If a medical problem is discovered, it will likely influence how potty training should proceed and must be thoroughly discussed with your health care professional. If a problem is not discovered, pack your bags and get ready to embark on the potty journey.

On the other hand, if your child stays dry through the night, he is exhibiting one of the two absolute signs of readiness for toilet training. Your child is definitely "ready," as mentioned above.

Child Has a Mental Age of 18-24 Months

Mental age is not the same as chronological age. Mental age refers to your child's intellectual development, as measured by a standard intelligence test. Test results are usually divided into verbal and nonverbal performance areas. Many children with autism have an uneven profile of development. For example, your child might score higher in areas such as motor skills and lower in other areas such as language. Some children have higher scores in performance areas like matching or problem solving than they do in verbal areas.

Your child's teacher or a psychologist can give you information about your child's mental age, if you are in doubt. Your health care provider may also be able to help supply this information.

Child Has Formed Bowel Movements

Regular, formed bowel movements indicate physical readiness for toilet training. The child with frequent loose stools should have a medical evaluation to determine the reason. Often loose stools are related to food intolerances or allergies that can be treated with diet or supplements. Sometimes more fiber must be introduced into the child's diet, or certain foods must be eliminated. It may be necessary to consult your child's health care provider. This area is discussed further in Chapter 10: *Other Bowel Training Obstacles and Predicaments.*

You Are Emotionally Ready

Related to the absence of stress – discussed further below – is the fact that you must be emotionally ready to set out upon and lead the potty journey. Toilet training most children with special needs is not easy. There are very few shortcuts. Time, commitment, and perseverance are necessary to apply the systematic methods and guided practice in this book. All of your partners on this journey (parents, teachers, and caregivers) must be ready to travel with you to ensure the trip will conclude successfully.

Child Is 4 Years Old

Once your child reaches 4 years of age, and there are no medical contraindications, you should begin planning the toileting journey if you have not already done so. After age 4, achieving continence should have the "right of way" over other skills and be a primary focus of educational and home intervention plans.

Absence of Physical Contraindication

This basically means the medical professionals agree that there is no medical reason not to begin toilet training.

Absence of Additional Stress

Major life events such as a move, newborn baby, major illness, job change, or divorce can cause significant strain to the family. If your family is undergoing a lot of stress at the time you are considering beginning to toilet train a child with special needs, especially a child with autism, you might be better off waiting until your family circumstances have stabilized.

Adding the commitment that toileting requires to an already stress-filled environment may intensify pressure and strain, causing unnecessary tension and anxiety. Indeed, it may be a set-up for toileting breakdown.

Well-meaning grandparents and friends who pressure you to start the journey before you are ready can also exacerbate stress. For everybody's sake, consider your situation and make a decision that, to all appearances, promises the greatest likelihood for success.

> **NOTE**: Some families elect to begin the toileting journey ahead of an anticipated major life change, such as the birth of a new baby, because they expect more confusion and disruption after the event occurs.

Which Direction First – Bladder or Bowel Training?

Choosing where to begin, with bladder or bowel training, is a personal decision.

Bowel

In some respects, beginning with bowel movements is attractive because they usually occur less often and, therefore, mean fewer trips to the toilet. This may be desirable for anxious children who are resistant to sitting or for those who dislike disrupting their favorite activities. Also, when bowel movements are regular, such as every morning or evening, they are more predictable, which makes it easier to determine when the child should sit on the toilet. In such cases, there is a greater likelihood that the child will figure out what you are asking her to do and that she will successfully defecate in the toilet. Beginning with bowel training means fewer new expectations for the child.

Finally, sometimes the signals indicating that a child is about to have a bowel movement are easily noticed. For example, the child may become very quiet, squat, stand still, hide, or get very red in the face.

Bladder

Beginning with urine training is also acceptable. If your child is dry through the night, shows an interest in the toilet, or brings you a clean diaper, you might elect to start with urine training. If the child has a predictable urination schedule and can stay dry for 2 hours you might also begin here.

Probably the biggest indicator of readiness is the willingness and ability of your crew (see Chapter 3) to invest the time and energy into this expedition. Everyone must be committed and expect to spend many hours on the journey. **After your child is 4 years old, don't spend a lot of time worrying about your child's readiness, but think about your own.**

Attending the toilet training workshop by Judy Coucouvanis was the best thing I could do for our family. I realized that my 6-year-old autistic son could be toilet trained with everyone who cares for him becoming a team when it came to being consistent in actions and words.

– Mother of a 6-year-old with autism

CHAPTER 3
PACKING YOUR BAGS

As most seasoned travelers know, the better prepared you are for the journey, the greater the likelihood the trip will be a smooth one. They also know that the more frequently you travel, the more comfortable you become with the routine of preparing and packing. Changes, delays, and setbacks, although unwelcome, are tackled with some degree of expertise.

The same is true for the toilet training journey. The better prepared you are, the greater likelihood of a smooth journey. Preparing for this trip requires assembling your toileting crew, deciding what language to use, establishing a documentation system, gathering supplies, and selecting rewards.

Toileting Crew

Although you are the potty tour director, you must enlist the help and support of a crew to assist you and your child on the trip. Ideally, your crew will consist of your spouse or significant other, your child's teacher(s), day care provider(s), family member(s) who have regular contact with the child, and your child's babysitters.

Along with you, your crew will be responsible for collecting data, accompanying your child into the bathroom, carrying out the toileting routine, and administering rewards. **They must follow the schedule without deviation unless you have agreed upon a change.**

Some crew members will be more experienced than others, and most will have opinions about how best to proceed. Keep the lines of communication open and encourage them to talk about their ideas and concerns with you. Enlist their help in problem solving and making the decisions described in the next several chapters. However, agree to adhere to the guidelines presented here

for best results. Consistency is absolutely essential. **Everybody must stick to the road map to make sure you reach the final destination safe and sound.**

Language: What to Say

Everyone who embarks on this journey with you and your child must speak the same language. Gather your crew together and, as a group, carefully choose the words you will use for toilet, body parts, urine, and bowel movements. Some common choices are:

- Toilet (potty, bathroom, pot, potty chair)
- Vagina (pee pee)
- Penis (wee wee, pee pee)
- Buttocks (butt, bottom, po-po)
- Urine (pee, wee)
- Bowel movements (BM, poop, poopy, kaka)

There are no right or wrong choices. It is a matter of personal preference and comfort. However, everyone should use the same word(s) to avoid confusing the child. Consider what will be easiest for your child to understand and the team to remember. You might also want to think about what you want your child to say as he ages ("toilet" may be more appropriate at age 9 than "potty"). In many cases, it is easier to start out with and stick to the term you ultimately wish the child to be familiar with and use.

In addition to the above decisions, come to an agreement on what to say to the child when it is time to use the bathroom. Again, everyone must use the same words every time to reduce misunderstanding. Some choices include the following:

- It's time to go potty.
- It's time to use the bathroom.
- It's time to go to the toilet.
- It's potty time.
- Let's go potty.
- It's time to try and pee.

For children who need visual communication in addition to, or instead of, verbal communication, you might choose to use the Mayer-Johnson Boardmaker (www. mayer-johnson.com) picture for toilet or take a photograph of the toilet the child will be using.

NOTE: Remember that children with autism and related disorders often have unique difficulties understanding speech and may require physical or visual communication aids in addition to verbal communication to help them understand what you are asking them to do. More about this in Chapter 7: *Final Preparations*.

Travel Records

Recording complete and accurate toileting information every day is indispensable to a successful toileting journey. The Daily Progress Record (see Appendix B) and the Travel Crew Journal (see Appendix D) portray essential details of the day to everyone. This kind of data collection and record keeping may sound difficult and overwhelming, but as you are about to see, it is actually very simple.

1. *Daily Progress Record*

The Daily Progress Record informs your toileting crew of the time of the child's scheduled trips to the toilet and shows the result of those trips to you and others. Like a daily journal, it is used to record your child's progress and setbacks. Anyone with knowledge about your child's successes or accidents must take responsibility for documenting results on the Daily Progress Record. **It is the most important tool of the toileting journey**. It becomes your road map and must be used each and every day until the trip is concluded. Without it, you and your team will become lost because you will not have vital data to guide your decisions.

How to use the Daily Progress Record. Using the Daily Progress Record is simple, whether you are experienced at record keeping or not. Write in the scheduled sitting times in the boxes at the top of the form (see page 28). You will learn how to determine these in Chapter 5: *Planning the Route*. Write the date under each numbered day. Indicate dry pants and accidents in the Pants column and toileting successes in the Toilet column by using this key: D = dry, U = urine, BM = bowel movement, U/BM = both urine and bowel movement, N = No results.

Sample Daily Progress Record

Scheduled Sitting Times: 7:30   9:00   11:30   1:30

Time	Day 1 Sun July 8 Pants	Toilet	Day 2 Mon July 9 Pants	Toilet	Day 3 Tues July 10 Pants	Toilet
Date						
7:00						
7:30	U	N	U	N	U	U
8:00						
8:30						
9:00	D	U	U	U	U/BM	U
9:30						
10:00						
10:30						
11:00						
11:30	U/BM	N	D	U	U	N
12:00						
12:30						
1:00			BM			
1:30	D	U	D	N	D	U

This record indicates that this child had wet pants at 7:30 in the morning on Day 1. He was dry and urinated in the toilet at 9:00. At 11:30 he had a urine and bowel accident, and at 1:30 he was dry and urinated in the toilet.

On Day 2, the child was wet at 7:30. He was wet again at 9:00 and also urinated in the toilet then and again at 11:30. He was soiled at 1:00 and was dry at 1:30, but did not urinate in the toilet.

On the third day, although he was wet at 7:30 a.m., he also urinated in the toilet. He had an accident at 9:00 and urinated in the toilet. At 11:30 he was wet again, and at 1:30 he was dry and also urinated in the toilet.

Such data for your child are absolutely critical when forming the trip schedule described in Chapter 5.

At the end of the week, record the total number of urine and bowel accidents and successes on the Progress Record for Month of ____ document found in Appendix C.

Progress Record for Month of _____ May _____

	Total Week 1	Total Week 2	Total Week 3	Total Week 4	TOTAL Month
Urine Accidents	42	35	28	21	126
Urine in Toilet	3	10	17	24	54
BM Accidents	7	6	7	5	25
BM in Toilet	0	1	0	2	3

This sample report shows us that as the weeks progress, this child is having fewer total urine accidents per week and more successes in the toilet. Once the next month's data are recorded, the hope is that you will note that the total number of monthly accidents are reduced while the total successes for the month have increased. This is *your* reinforcement that what you are doing is working!

2. *Travel Crew Journal*

The Travel Crew Journal may be copied on to the reverse side of the Daily Progress Record to make it easier to keep everything together. It is used for communication between crew members and the tour director. It is the place to write down questions, record any problems, note special events such as field trips, or write about "special moments."

Date/Name	Sample Entry in Travel Crew Journal
7/8 Mary	Lots of gas today, need more pull-ups. Likes the new books!
7/8 Jack	First BM tonight in the potty !!!!!

Clothing

Loose-fitting clothing without zippers or snaps is easiest for your child to pull up and down with minimal or no assistance. Elastic waistbands are often best. Try to avoid one-piece outfits, overalls, and buttons.

Now is the time to support your child in developing independent dressing and undressing skills. Often parents decide to teach dressing skills while they are contemplating a child's readiness to begin toileting. I recommend teaching dressing in advance as it helps to remove one barrier to independent toileting.

Supplies/Setting up the Bathroom

No trip would be complete without the proper provisions. In this case, we are talking toilet seat, footstool, timer, books and toys, and rewards.

Toilet Seat

The type of toilet seat to use is determined by the size of the child and his physical limitations, if any. Sometimes children with autism and related disorders – due to their desire for routine and sameness – have difficulty transitioning to a typical toilet if they have been using a separate potty chair. For this reason, I recommend using a child-sized toilet seat that fits on top of the bathroom toilet at home. These can be purchased from most major department or variety stores.

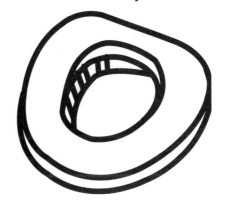

You might also purchase a portable toilet seat to carry with you into public restrooms. Schools and day care settings often have child-sized toilets that are low to the floor and that children are able to sit comfortably on. Check to see and make plans to bring your child's toilet seat, if necessary.

If your child is sensitive to a hard, plastic toilet seat, consider padding it or lining it with soft fabric such as flannel. The padding or fabric can be attached to the underside of the seat with Velcro, thus making it easy to remove for washing.

Places that supply special commodes and adaptive equipment for children with physical limitations may be found on the Resource List at the end of this book.

Footstool

While sitting on the toilet, the child must feel comfortable and secure with her feet firmly supported. If her feet do not touch the floor, place a step stool under her feet. A block of wood, a cardboard box, or a plastic container may also be used. She must feel safe and balanced so that she can relax and concentrate on eliminating in the toilet. If her back is unsupported, roll up a large bath towel and place it behind her.

Timer

A timer is necessary to signal when each trip to the toilet begins and ends. If your child needs to learn to sit on the toilet, plan to purchase a digital timer (see Chapter 6: *Avoiding Disaster*). Timers are available in the kitchen supply department of your favorite variety store.

Activities

As for any road trip, plan activities to be used along the way. Select a variety of washable books and toys that can remain in the bathroom for your child to use while sitting on the toilet. The activities should interest and relax the child, but not require so much focus that he does not concentrate on what he is supposed to be doing. Placing an interest-ing poster on the wall can also help to prolong attention.

Some parents rotate toys in and out of the bathroom on a regular basis to maintain their child's interest and motivation. If you do not provide activities that keep little hands occupied, you may find your child playing with the toilet paper, toilet water, or even his genitals. So prepare ahead of time.

Rewards

Any behavior that happens before a reward is delivered is more likely to occur again. This common principle of behavior modification is the reason to use rewards with your child. Think of it this way. Your boss wants you to use a new computer-generated checklist every time you complete a sale. She informs you that every time you complete the new checklist, you will receive a 10-dollar bonus. Most of us will figure out pretty quickly how to complete the new checklist and try to generate sales.

The same is true of our children. When a child knows he will receive a favorite treat or get to do a preferred activity, he will be more willing to try to do what you ask. We want the child to figure out how to eliminate in the toilet and stay dry between sittings as quickly as possible. Using rewards helps your child do this. More about this in Chapter 4: *Travelers' Compensation: Using Rewards.*

Potty Journey Countdown

A final tool to get ready for the trip is the Potty Journey Countdown. Located in Appendix E, it is a checklist of the essentials you need to prepare for your journey. It includes a timeline of what to do starting two months before the journey and ending during the trip. Its components will be explained in the remainder of this guidebook.

CHAPTER 4
TRAVELERS'[19] COMPENSATION
Using Rewards

The most important traveler on this journey, your child, will require some recognition and compensation for his efforts. After all, you will be asking him to attempt something that may not be easy, and you want him to succeed.

Choosing a Reward

Choose a powerful reward. This means picking an activity, small snack, or object that you know your child especially likes. The reward is something that you know he will work to receive. Talk with your child's teachers, care providers, and your toileting crew to share ideas. The Traveler's Reward Survey presented in Appendix F may help you discover potential rewards that you have not thought of before. **School, home, and day care do not have to use the same reward(s).**

Erica likes to play with rubber snakes. Her mother takes a trip to the dollar store and purchases a bag of snakes.

Sam likes to look at photographs. His mother collects all the family photo albums and puts them into a special box. She also downloads Sam's favorite photos onto her cell phone for immediate use in public bathrooms.

Devon likes all kinds of candy. His mother collects an assortment of small candies and places them inside a transparent container that she keeps in the bathroom.

Praise and other forms of social attention, such as hugs, kisses, high-fives, and cheering, are also powerful rewards and should be used liberally. Tell your child what he is doing right; he is doing a good job sitting on the potty. Tell him how proud you are when he pees in the potty.

Most children like attention and will work hard to get it. If your child does not respond to or like praise and social attention (perhaps due to an autism spectrum disorder), reward with a preferred activity or special treat, and calmly tell the child what he did right, "Good job peeing in the potty."

Be careful not to inadvertently reinforce your child with negative attention. Negative attention includes an angry or frustrated facial expression, scolding, pleading, or yelling. It is natural for parents to want to scold after the child has an accident, but be very careful how you do this. Despite what many believe, negative attention is not a punishment! It is a reward, and it can reinforce behavior, especially if it is the only type of attention your child receives.

Some children love to watch their parents get angry, while others love the sound of an angry voice. If this is the case for your child, be certain that you keep your face and voice tone calm and matter-of-fact.

 NOTE: Positive attention for what your child is doing right and little to no attention for what she is doing wrong are the best social reinforcement strategies.

Amount of Reward

The reward you choose should be given out in small amounts. This helps encourage your child to continue trying while not getting tired of or bored with the reward. Below are some suggested quantities.

Type of Reward	Amount
Candies	2-3 M&Ms or Skittles, 1 candy kiss
Snacks	One very small cookie, 2 crackers or chips
Drink	1 oz.
Television show/movie/computer time	5-10 minutes (use a timer)
Favorite activity (water play, blowing bubbles, music)	5-10 minutes (use a timer)
Story/art project	One story/art project

Access to Reward

Limit access to the reward. This means the reward is saved for toileting, and the child may not have it at other times during the day.

Sarah earns 5 minutes of the Weather Channel – her favorite interest – every time she urinates in the toilet. She can only watch the Weather Channel after she urinates in the toilet.

Reward Conditions

Give the reward contingent upon the desired behavior. This means that the reward is only given when the child meets the current expected conditions.

Miguel earns a small cookie when he urinates in the toilet. If he does not urinate during one of his scheduled sitting times, he does not earn the cookie, even if his mother thinks he was especially cooperative. He receives the reward *only* when he urinates in the toilet.

Sometimes the child may ask for the reward at other times during the day. Simply let him know what he needs to do in order to receive it.

Aaron earns one teaspoon of frozen yogurt every time he urinates in the toilet. One day he asks his mom for yogurt when it is not time to sit on the toilet. She correctly tells him, "First pee in the potty, then you can have yogurt."

Aaron goes into the bathroom and urinates in the toilet. His mother rewards him with a teaspoon of yogurt. Soon he begins to initiate going to the bathroom on his own because he wants yogurt. He might only urinate a few drops, but his mother rewards him because she recognizes his behavior as progress in learning this new skill.

It is not uncommon for children to begin to initiate going into the bathroom by themselves. Do not make your child wait for a scheduled sitting trip if he tries to go potty on his own. Praise his self-initiation and reward his success. In addition, do not insist that your child come and get you before going to the bathroom. Your ultimate goal is independent toileting, and if you insist that your child come and get you first, you are adding a step that requires dependence upon you. It is much better that your child has access to the bathroom, walks there alone, and then you enter if needed. Once he is in the bathroom, you can teach him to ask for help by ringing a bell or calling for you if you are not aware that he is there.

You will need to be extra observant during the first few weeks that you implement this program. Stop what you are doing and follow your child if you think he is going into the bathroom so that you can praise him immediately for his efforts.

Reward Frequency

Give the reward **every time.** When you first start toilet training, the reward must be given every time the child meets the current expectation.

Mark's favorite activity was visiting the car wash, and his mother considered driving through the car wash as a reward when Mark urinated in the toilet. However, she realized she could not drive through the car wash every time he urinated in the toilet.

This reward was not a good choice when beginning the potty journey, but might be used later after Mark is successfully urinating in the toilet and is being rewarded for staying dry for longer periods of time. Early on, a better choice is a treat or brief activity he can do immediately at home.

Variety of Rewards

It is a good strategy to vary the rewards. Your child may tire after a few days of the reward you have chosen, so it is best to have a variety of rewards on hand. This will help her continue to stay interested and motivated to try and succeed. If you are using snacks, keep an assortment of favorite snacks available to choose from.

Reward Posters

Make a reward poster. It demonstrates for the child what to do and describes the consequences for when he does it. As illustrated, the first part of the poster presents a picture of a child sitting on the toilet. If needed, take a photograph of your child sitting on the toilet. Some children understand Boardmaker (www.mayer-johnson.com) or pictures available from the Internet. The picture is followed by an equals symbol (=). A representation of the reward follows. If your child will earn a snack, place the snack wrapping paper, container, or a photo of the snack on the poster.

When you change the reward, also change the poster. If the child has a choice of rewards, illustrate the choices on the poster.

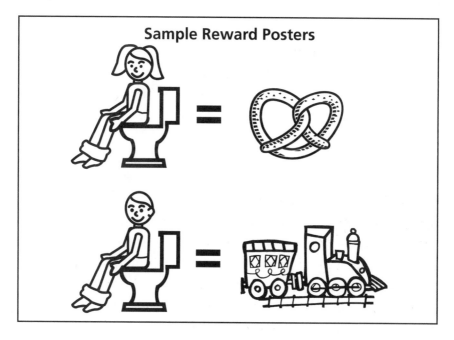

Sample Reward Posters

More Thoughts About Rewards

For some children, a part of the toileting routine, such as flushing the toilet or washing hands (water play), might be a reward. Go ahead and use it as a reward as long as you follow the guidelines above.

NOTE: If you decide to use washing hands as the reward, use wipes, a wet wash cloth, or paper towels at other times of the day when your child needs to "wash hands." This way you save the most "powerful" reward – washing hands with running water – for toileting only.

Andrew (age 3-1/2 with possible AS) was motivated by M&Ms, but no matter how many times I reminded him of the reward, he was only willing to "go" after holding it for sometimes up to eight hours!

After attending Judy Coucouvanis' toilet training lecture, I printed pictures of a toilet, an equal sign, and an M&M picture from the Internet. I taped them to the wall directly across from the toilet. I explained to him that he had to "put something into the toilet to get the M&Ms."

Within two weeks, Andrew was fully toilet trained! Apparently, it's true that most children, especially those with special needs, respond better to visual cues than to verbal ones. He started keeping his pull-ups dry all night and was doing the bowel movements in the toilet, too. Within a month, he told me that he wanted to start standing up to pee and never really had another accident!

Maybe part of the success came from Mommy relaxing about it, since I felt relieved to finally have some great tools. I also utilized the chart to track how often he was "going." That probably helped me too, since you might remember all of the toileting details over the course of a day, but not much beyond that. Also, it was great for monitoring constipation issues!

Andrew did have some relapses a few months later when he had a cold, but only with bowel movement accidents. I rewarded him with M&Ms or special videos only when he kept clean for a long period of time, which seemed to work, but it took a couple of months after the regression. I think he didn't want to stop playing to go to the bathroom; he also had some constipation issues.

– Lisa Carleton, Troy, MI

CHAPTER 5
PLANNING THE ROUTE

N
ow that you are prepared for the journey, you are ready to begin planning the specific route that you will take. To do this, you will need to discover your child's present toileting habits – the times each day she is most likely to wet or soil her diaper. **Do not skip this step**. It is the first and most critical step of your journey. You will need the Daily Progress Record (DPR) from Appendix B.

Discovering Your Child's Present Toileting Habits

On the first day, check the child when he first gets up in the morning. Is his diaper wet, dry, or soiled? Record your findings on the DPR in the Pants column. Change his diaper. Check him again one hour later and every hour thereafter until he goes to bed. Always record the results on the DPR. Baker and Brightman (1989) recommend recording this information for two weeks.

In general, I agree with their recommendation. However, there are occasions when a pattern (discussed below) is discovered after one week. In those situations, collecting a second week of data is usually unnecessary. If you are unsure, collect two weeks of data.

Elicit the support of teachers, day care providers, and anyone else who might be checking/changing your child's diapers during this two-week period. Send a copy of the DPR with the child so your team can document hourly directly onto it. Or ask them to write down separate notes and then transfer the data onto the DPR at home.

Because of the very absorbent nature of today's diapers, it is often difficult to tell when the child has urinated. Some parents elect to put underwear beneath the diaper so that it is easier to tell when a child is wet. Others place a thin sanitary pad inside the diaper for the same reason. Still others use training pants with plastic pants over them.

A less traditional approach for children who have difficulty sensing when they are wet or even damp is illustrated in the following.

Our daughter has a diagnosis of 22q13 (Deletion Syndrome) and, as a result, the effectiveness of her nerve system is reduced. Often she would hold her urine with only a few drops soiling, so when we asked if she was dry, it was very difficult for her to notice. She began to feel it was a safety net. Judy's suggestion of wearing a skirt without underwear at home made our daughter really focus on making it to the toilet in time. It has been very successful.

– Parents of 3-year-old Amelia

Change the underwear, pad, training pants, or pull-ups every time your child is wet or soiled. Remember, the DPR is the most important tool of your toileting journey, so it must be completed every hour.

Plotting the Course:
Determining the Schedule

While you are collecting information about your child's current elimination habits, do not change any of her daily routines. Do not offer more or less to eat or drink or expect her to use the toilet. **Simply collect the data so that you can eventually set up a schedule that is right for her.**

If your child had been sitting on the toilet occasionally prior to this step, it is O.K. for him to continue to do so. While you are collecting these data is a good time for your child to get extra practice pulling his pants up and down.

Once you have two weeks of information on the DPR, begin to look for patterns. A pattern is a consistent time when urination or defecation is most likely to occur. To determine this, mark all "U's" using a highlighter pen in one color and all "BM's" in another color.

Daily Progress Record for Katie

Time	Day 1 Pants	Toilet	Day 2 Pants	Toilet	Day 3 Pants	Toilet	Day 4 Pants	Toilet	Day 5 Pants	Toilet	Day 6 Pants	Toilet	Day 7 Pants	Toilet
Date	6/19 Thurs		6/20 Fri		6/21 Sat		6/22 Sun		6/23 Mon		6/24 Tues		6/25 Wed	
6:00														
6:30														
7:00														
7:30														
8:00													U	
8:30	U		U											
9:00					U				U		U			
9:30	D		U		U				BM					
10:00							U				U		U	
10:30	D		D		U		U							
11:00									D		U		U	
11:30	U/BM		U		D		U							
12:00									U		U			
12:30														
1:00	D		U		D		U/BM						U	
1:30					U/BM				U/BM		D			
2:00	D		BM				U						D	
2:30					D				U		U			
3:00	U		D				D						D	
3:30					U				U		U			
4:00	U		D				U							
4:30					D				U		D			U
5:00	U		U											
5:30					U				U		U			
6:00	U													
6:30			BM		U		U		U/BM				U	
7:00	U										BM			
7:30			U		U				D		U			
8:00							U							
8:30	BM		D						U				U	
9:00	U		U				U							

49

What do we know about Katie by looking at the one-week record on page 49?

- She has fairly regular bowel movements, usually after lunch and again in the evening.
- There is no real pattern to her urination.
- She is frequently wet – often on an hourly basis – but has occasional periods where she stays dry for 3 hours.
- She urinated in the toilet once during one of her occasional trips to the bathroom.

If you see a regular bowel pattern emerging in the data for your child, set the toileting time 15 minutes prior to that time. In Katie's case, because she usually has a bowel movement between 1 and 2 p.m., she would sit on the toilet for a BM at 12:45.

When you see a regular urine pattern, the toileting schedule should follow the same pattern. If there is no regular urine pattern, as for Katie, the first toileting time is when the child first gets up in the morning, and then every **1½-2 hours** afterwards. We would not sit Katie every hour because we do not want to encourage her to urinate every hour; we want to teach her to start to hold and urinate a minimum of every 1½-2 hours. Let's look at another example.

Daily Progress Record for Aaron

	Day 1		Day 2		Day 3		Day 4		Day 5		Day 6		Day 7	
Date	1/18	Mon	1/19	Tues	1/20	Wed	1/21	Thurs	1/22	Fri	1/23	Sat	1/24	Sun
Time	Pants	Toilet	Pants	Toilet	Pants	Toilet	Pants	Toilet	Pants	Toilet	Pants	Toilet	Pants	Toilet
6:00														
6:30														
7:00														
7:30														
8:00	D		D		D		D							
8:30									U					
9:00	U		D		D		D				D		D	
9:30			U				U							
10:00	U		BM		U		D		D		U/BM		U	
10:30	BM													
11:00	D		D		U/BM		D		U		D		UBM	
11:30														
12:00	D		D		D		D		D		D		D	
12:30														
1:00	D		D		D		D		D		U		D	
1:30							U/BM							
2:00	D		D		D		D		D		D		D	
2:30														
3:00	U		D		D		D		D		D		D	
3:30			U/BM		U				U					
4:00	BM		BM				U				U		U	
4:30	U				BM									
5:00	D		D		D		D		D		D		D	
5:30														
6:00	D		D		U/BM		D		D		D		D	
6:30														
7:00	U		U		D		D		D		D		U/BM	
7:30							U							
8:00	D		D		D		D		D		U		U	
8:30	U		U		U				BM					
9:00	U						D							

In this example, we see a definite pattern.

- Aaron usually awakens dry.
- He does not urinate or have a BM in his diaper during afternoon preschool. On Thursday, Day 4, there was no school, and he urinated at home. His diapers are always wet when he comes home from preschool.
- He is capable of holding urine for many hours.

Based upon these data, Aaron's scheduled trips to the toilet would be as follows: immediately upon arising from bed, 9:45 a.m., 11 a.m., 1 p.m., immediately before he leaves preschool, immediately when he gets home from preschool, or 3:30 p.m., 7 p.m., and 8:30 p.m.

At first, record keeping seems a bit tedious, but in the end it is useful, insightful, and helpful in establishing a successful routine for toileting. Judy's methodical approach is really common sense, but is necessary for those of us who seem to have lost that common sense somewhere along the line. Judy has been a key component in my daughter's ability to become a "big girl" with toileting.

– Mother of 11-year-old nonverbal daughter with special needs

CHAPTER 6
AVOIDING DISASTER

nce you make the decision to set out on the toileting journey, you want the trip to go as smoothly as possible, and for your child to be successful. To do this, you need to watch out for and avoid disasters and heartbreaks. Potential disaster comes in the form of the child who will not sit on the toilet co-operatively.

Some children refuse outright to sit on the toilet. They whine, cry, scream, or even hit and kick. Others sit for a few seconds and then jump off. Still others become rigid and stiff as a board, using super-human strength to keep from sitting.

There is usually a reason for such dramatic responses. Some children are afraid of the toilet. They do not understand its purpose, fear falling off, or are uncomfortable sitting upon it. The seat may be too cold, too hard, or too soft. The stool may be too large, and without sufficient support the child fears she will fall in. Others resist because the request to sit on the toilet is a change in routine. Some don't understand what you are asking. Still others tantrum at most any request, including an appeal to sit on the toilet.

If any of these characteristics describes your child, do not despair. You can take a temporary, but essential, detour in the toileting journey to teach your child to sit on the potty and thereby avoid disaster.

Practice Trips: Teaching Your Child to Sit

Think of it this way. You have been asked to take a cross-country bike trip in three months with friends. You haven't ridden a bicycle in 20 years and need to relearn how to ride. So you set up a program to practice in preparation for the trip. Here's what's needed to help your child practice her new skill.

Supplies

You will need the toilet training supplies described in Chapters 3 and 4. In addition, if your child is sensitive to cold objects, consider lining the toilet seat with warm fabric, such as fleece or flannel. If your child prefers a soft cushion, consider purchasing a padded seat. A digital timer will be needed in all settings where the child is practicing. Finally, gather a small supply of books and toys for the child to play with.

Sam is 4 years old and has autism. He screams whenever anyone tries to put him on the toilet. His mother finds a padded toilet seat that fits on the toilet and a small stool where his feet can rest. She also has a rolled-up towel available to support his back.

Timing

Establish six to eight times to "practice" sitting on the toilet every day. The practice times can take place at your convenience, as the child is not expected to eliminate in the toilet, simply to practice sitting on it.

Work with school and child care staff to determine when some of the practice times can occur in those settings. An adult will need to accompany the child to the bathroom and stay with him, so see what is a workable schedule.

Sam's parents both work. Sam goes to special education preschool in the morning and to day care in the afternoon. His toilet crew decides that he will practice sitting on the toilet at home at 7 a.m., 5 p.m., and 8 p.m. He will practice in preschool at 8:30 a.m. and 10:30 a.m. He will practice in day care at 1 p.m. and 3:30 p.m. Sam uses a picture schedule at school, so a picture of a toilet was added to his schedule.

Rewards

Choose a powerful reward. As described in Chapter 4, rewards are used to try to motivate the child to do what you are asking. In this case, because your child does not sit on the toilet willingly, you must encourage him with something very powerful, something that he really likes.

Sam loves chocolate. His team gathers a supply of M&Ms, candy kisses, chocolate pudding, and chocolate candy bars. The team also makes reward posters for Sam and keeps one in each bathroom. The reward choice for the day is attached to the poster with Velcro.

Sam's Reward Poster

NOTE: To begin, some parents show the child the poster and explain in advance what will happen. Some add a picture of a toilet to the child's schedule if the child uses a schedule. Others just begin. There is no one correct way here. You know best your child's communication abilities; use the type of communication and schedule you are using for other areas of daily life to explain what is happening.

Practice Sessions

When the time to practice arrives, say to the child, "It is time to sit on the toilet (potty)." **Do not ask the child if he wants to sit on the potty, is ready to sit on the potty, or would like to sit on the potty. Simply tell him it is time to sit. Do not say "O.K.?"**

Take the child into the bathroom. Show her the poster and remind her of the reward. Sit the child on the toilet and kneel or stand in front of her, gently holding her if needed. Set the timer for **5 seconds**. Some parents count out loud, "5, 4, 3, 2, 1." When the timer rings, immediately praise the child, "Good sitting on the potty," and give her the reward.

It is common for a child to be uncooperative the first few days of practice sessions. Give the reward anyway in the beginning. The progressive sequence is as follows:
- gently hold your child for the 5 seconds
- gradually remove your grasp (inches at a time)
- stand up
- slowly back up

This may take several days of 5-second practice sessions to achieve.

When the child can sit alone on the toilet without crying or screaming, and you can be in the room about 2 feet away, she is considered cooperative. Some children accomplish this within a day or two of 6-8 practice sessions, others take several days.

Once she is cooperative, add 5 more seconds to the timer the next day and expect her to sit willingly for 10 seconds before she receives the reward. Stay at 10 seconds for all practice sessions that day. If she is cooperative for at least 75% of the practice sessions for that day, increase to 15 seconds the next day.

Practice Sessions	
Number of Practice Sessions/Day	**Number of Cooperative Sessions Needed/Day**
8	6
7	5
6	4

Continue to add 5-10 seconds per day if the child is co-operative for at least 75% of the previous day's sessions. The above chart tells you how many sessions that will be. If the child starts to resist, stay at the current practice session length until she is successful before increasing it.

Remember, the child does not receive a reward if she is uncooperative (gets off the toilet, cries, screams, strikes at you, etc.) once you have moved beyond 5 seconds. Do not scold or threaten her. Simply say something like, "I'm sure you will do better next time. Remember to stay on the toilet (stay calm, quiet, etc.)."

If the child unexpectedly urinates or has a BM in the toilet during a practice sitting, praise him, give him a bonus reward, and let him get up before the timer rings. Record the child's progress on the Sitting Practice Record in Appendix G. This chart will help you and your crew know exactly where to start each day. For urine training, the goal is **3 minutes of independent, cooperative sitting**. Once this goal is achieved, you are ready to resume the toileting journey.

Sitting Practice Record						
Date: <u>October 12</u>		Day: <u>3</u>		Day of Week: <u>Tuesday</u>		
TIME	Pull-Up/Diaper D/U/BM	TOILET D/U/BM	# SEC./MIN.	COOPERATION (YES) (NO)	REWARD	NOTES
7 AM	D = U	T = D	20 seconds	Yes	Cocoa Puffs	Tired
8:30 AM	D = U	T = D	20 seconds	No	None	Cried and tried to get off
10:30 AM	D = D	T = D	20 seconds	Yes	M&Ms	Happy
1 PM	D = U	T = D	20 seconds	Yes	Candy kiss	A little fussy
3:30 PM	D = D	T = D	20 seconds	Yes	Chocolate cookie	Great job
5 PM	D = U	T = D	20 seconds	No	None	Tantrum
8 PM	D = U	T = D	20 seconds	Yes	Chocolate pudding	Much better

In this example, Sam was cooperative for the required five practice sittings, so he will increase to 30-second sittings on Day 4. If he had been uncooperative three or more times, he would stay at 20 seconds for Day 4.

NOTE: Teaching your child to sit on the toilet can occur simultaneously with collecting information about current toileting habits, where you are checking her hourly to see if she is wet/dry/soiled.

Some children already know how to sit on the toilet for a short time, such as 30 seconds, before starting to fuss or trying to get off. If this is your child, increase the amount of the first practice session to the length of time that your child usually sits willingly. If this is 30 seconds, start at 30 seconds; if it is 1 minute, start at 1 minute. Then increase by 15 seconds a day as described until the child sits for 3 minutes cooperatively.

Alex, age 6, had never "eliminated" in the toilet. We worked through the 3 minutes on the toilet at home and at school with rewards, and he learned it quickly. Then, last week, with Potty Scotty* and the patience of my wonderful educational assistants, Alex urinated in the toilet for the first time EVER! He's been using the toilet ever since, and even though he's had a few accidents, he is very much on his way to being trained. He got big rewards and lots of praise and is doing well at home, too.

Tara C. Tuchel, autism specialist

* Potty Scotty is an anatomically correct drink-and wet-on-demand boy doll.

CHAPTER 7
FINAL PREPARATIONS

We are now ready to make the final preparations for the journey. Because toileting is a
lifelong skill that has very few variations once
learned, it is important to teach the toileting routine correctly from beginning to end. If you do so, you are not
likely to have to re-teach it later.

Establishing a Toileting Routine

A typical toileting routine for girls without physical limitations is:

1. Enter the bathroom
2. Close the door
3. Pull down pants
4. Sit on the toilet
5. Urinate or defecate in the toilet
6. Take toilet paper and wipe (front to back)
7. Flush
8. Pull up pants
9. Wash hands
10. Dry hands
11. Open the door

While most boys eventually learn to stand to urinate, it is often better that they sit when they begin training. Once they have figured out how to have a BM in the toilet, they can usually be taught to stand up to urinate quite easily. If your son has not yet learned to defecate or urinate in the toilet, I encourage you to have him sit when he first begins the journey to avoid confusion later.

Visual Supports

Many children with special needs are visual learners and are helped when they can *see* what is expected of them. For this reason, it is often very helpful to show the toileting routine in picture form. Each part of the routine is photographed or illustrated using commercial illustrations, such as those pictures or symbols available from Mayer-Johnson (see Resources and References).

Toileting Routine

1. Enter the bathroom.

2. Close the door.

3. Pull down pants.

4. Sit down on the toilet.

5. Pee/Poop in the toilet.

6. Take toilet paper and wipe.

7. Flush one time.

8. Pull up pants.

9. Wash hands.

10. Dry hands.

11. Open the door.

If you choose to take photographs, be sure to focus on only one step of the routine in each photo; for example, washing hands. Make the primary focus of the step very clear. For example, the photograph should show her hands under a running faucet or the child's head and torso with her hands under the running faucet instead of the entire bathroom. (See also the example Toileting Routine in Appendix H.)

The pictures should be clearly visible to the child while he is in the bathroom. You do not want to have to repeatedly tell your child what to do and eventually want him to use the bathroom independently. The pictures (or written words if your child can read) help your child remember the routine. They might be sequenced on a shower door, wall, or mirror. They could also be placed in a book, such as a photo album, or on a poster. A clipboard is another option.

Some Options for Setting up the Support

- Use Velcro to secure each picture to poster board or a file folder. After each step of the routine is finished, the child removes the picture of the completed step and puts it into an envelope. Then he checks to see the next step.

NOTE: It is your job to reorder the pictures after the child is finished.

- Have the child move a piece of Velcro, self-sticking paper, or a colored circle down the routine as each step is completed.

- Keep a pencil near a written schedule on a clipboard. The child checks or crosses off each step as he finishes it.

You may have to try out a few different systems before you hit upon the right one for your child. But remember, your goal is independent toileting, so you need to fade your verbal prompts and physical presence as soon as possible.

Fading your prompts and presence means that you gradually remove yourself from the bathroom. If you teach your child to use the pictures, the pictures will tell him what to do, so that you don't have to tell him. They will remind your child what to do when you are no longer there.

Issues Unique to Boys

Some boys do not know how to hold down their penis so that the urine flows into the toilet. Initially, you might place a towel over the boy's lap to absorb any overflow. Some boys can straddle the toilet. For others, you have to teach them to hold their penis down. Do this by gently putting your hand on top of the child's hand that is on top of his penis. Gradually remove your hand while praising the child.

Visuals were most helpful. A small-size poster board that I placed on the wall next to the toilet listing each step worked the best at age 7. He had these steps memorized for years, even when the poster was no longer up on the wall. Patience and consistency are also important.

– Mother of a 16-year-old son with autism

CHAPTER 8
LET'S "GO POTTY"

By now you have spent many hours, perhaps days, preparing for this moment – the first day of the toileting journey. You have the supplies you need, your schedule for the day, and your crew to assist you, so we're ready to go.

Urination Journey

At the first regularly scheduled sitting time, based upon the schedule you decided upon in Chapter 5, say the words to your child that you and your team have agreed to use, such as: "It's potty time." Supplement with a picture of the toilet, if needed to let the child know that the toilet trip is starting. Do *not* ask the child if she needs to use the toilet. You are the potty trip director, and it is time for your child to try to go to the bathroom.

Visual Schedules

For children who use a visual schedule to help them to understand what is happening next, make sure that toilet is on the schedule at the appropriate time. Direct the child to "check schedule" and follow whatever schedule-changing practices you have in place.

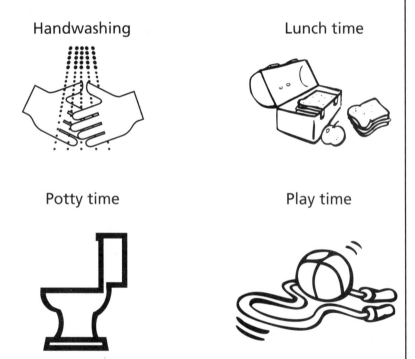

Handwashing

Lunch time

Potty time

Play time

---

1. Bring your child into the bathroom
2. Show him the toileting poster (see Chapter 4: *Travelers' Compensation*).
3. Guide him through the entire toileting routine as described in Chapter 7: *Final Preparations*.
4. Have the child sit on the toilet for 3 minutes. Use a timer to indicate for both you and the child when the time begins and ends. While he is sitting, the child may look at books, listen to music, or play with the special bathroom toys you have collected.
5. Stay in the bathroom with the child and praise him, "Good sitting on the potty!"
6. Clearly and simply explain what is expected. "Pee in the potty, then …" (ice cream, bubbles, or whatever the reward is). Point to the appropriate item on the poster.
7. Praise the child if she eliminates in the toilet. Let her stand up and give her the reward immediately.
8. Finish the routine and record the results on the Daily Progress Record (U – urine, BM – bowel movement, N – nothing). If the reward is an activity, such as watching a movie, finish the routine before giving her the reward.

 NOTE: Do not insist that she sit for 3 minutes if she urinates into the toilet before the time is up.

9. If the child does not eliminate in the toilet, remove her from the toilet when the time is up and finish the routine. Do not make her sit longer. The child does not earn a reward. Do not scold, lecture, or punish. You might say something like, "Maybe next trip you will pee in the potty and earn a ___" (reward). Record the results on the Daily Progress Record and sit her again at the **next scheduled sitting time** unless she indicates she needs to go to the bathroom before then.

Bonus Trips

If your child asks for her reward between trips to the potty, say something like, "First pee in the potty, then (reward)," and ask her if she would like to try to pee in the potty. If she says no, take her at the next planned sitting time. If she says yes, take her into the bathroom and follow the entire routine. If she urinates, enthusiastically praise her, give her the reward, and complete the routine. Record this extra trip and the results on the Daily Progress Record. Take her again at the next scheduled trip.

Follow the Route – No Bypasses!

If the child does not ask for the reward or does not indicate he needs to use the bathroom, stick to the schedule and take him again at the next sitting time. **Follow the planned potty trip times for one week before changing the times to fit the child's urination pattern more closely.**

Monica's scheduled sitting time at day care was 4:30 p.m. Her childcare provider faithfully took her every day at 4:30 p.m. for one week. Monica never urinated into the toilet. Instead, she usually had an accident just before 5 p.m. As a result, Monica's potty team decided to change the regularly scheduled sitting time to 4:50 p.m.

As illustrated in the following example, sometimes it is tempting to try to "guess" when the child will urinate, bypass the schedule, and take the child to the toilet without any real evidence to support the change. This veering off course may ultimately result in lost time and an extended journey.

Carter's scheduled sitting times were at 4:30 p.m. and 6:30 p.m. When his mother took him to the bathroom at 4:30 p.m., he did not urinate. The next night she decided to take him at 5:00 p.m. When he pulled down his pants, she discovered that he had already had an accident. The third night she took him at 4:45 p.m. He was dry, but he did not urinate in the toilet. She decided to take him again at 5:30 p.m.

The problem with this approach is that Carter's mother is not following the schedule as dictated by the data she and her team spent two weeks collecting. Because she is always "guessing" what to do, she may eventually fail in her efforts at toilet training. Certainly, she is trying to "catch" her son on time and is deviating from the schedule to try to accomplish this. It is common to be tempted to stray from the schedule without waiting one week. DO NOT DO THIS.

The most common reason for lack of success on the potty journey is failure to develop a good toileting schedule and remain with it. Only change the schedule once the Daily Progress Records consistently indicate there is a more accurate trip time than the one you have chosen.

Frequently Asked Questions (FAQs)

When Does My Child Start to Wear Underwear?

A: Once your child begins to urinate in the toilet, she should begin to dress in underwear, either alone or beneath her pull-up. She should no longer wear diapers except at night. If she resists wearing underwear, have her slip them on for short periods of time only, perhaps 5 minutes out of every 2 hours. Gradually increase the time she wears them until she is comfortable wearing them all day.

Sometimes adults are reluctant for the child to start using underwear because of the extra time and work involved. However, it is important that children begin to feel what it is like to be wet. If you wish to postpone the use of underwear a bit longer, place a panty liner inside the pull-up. It is not as absorbent as the pull-up, and the child should feel some wetness after an accident.

Should My Son Stand or Sit to Urinate?

A: If your son is not bowel trained, he should sit to urinate when you first start training. If he begins training by standing, he may have difficulty mastering bowel training. Some boys resist sitting once they have learned to stand. This makes bowel training much harder. Once your son has mastered defecating in the toilet, you can easily teach him how to stand. Some boys learn to "aim" by the use of a toilet target, such as a piece of cereal or a flushable "toilet-time target" purchased from www.WeBehave.com.

Max, age 8, (who was not even sitting on the toilet before) worked through his 3 minutes of sitting, and then we moved on to the reward for urinating only. I bought a doll called Potty Scotty that has real body parts to urinate out of. I was hoping to help make the connection for Max and another student. With the use of the doll, visual supports, and country magazines for rewards, Max urinated in the toilet for the first time yesterday!!! It was so exciting. He has had accidents since then, but we are going to keep trying. Yay!

Aaron, age 8, had been almost trained last year until he broke his foot and reverted back to pull-ups. We switched to just underwear at school, and he has been successful. I think the pull-up gives him the comfort to be lazy and urinate in his pants. He rarely has accidents at school any more and wears underwear all day every day (at school).

THANKS for everything! We are well on the way to very successful toilet training.

– Tara C. Tuchel, autism specialist

Bowel Journey

The bowel journey is the same as the urination journey, with the following changes:

- The time to sit the child on the toilet is 15 minutes before the time he usually has a BM. The schedule is based upon the data you have recorded on the Daily Progress Record. It consists of those times when BM's are most likely to occur; that is, the times with the highest totals during the data-collection period.

- Sit the child on the toilet for 10 minutes (use a timer). Take a 20-minute timed break. Sit him again for a second time for 10 minutes if he did not have a BM during the first 10-minute sitting period.

- Keep the child close to the bathroom, if possible, during the 20-minute break and observe him for any signs that he may need to have a BM, such as straining or squatting. Take him to the toilet immediately when you see such signals and start the second sitting time, even if 20 minutes have not passed.

- Change soiled diapers in the bathroom, the place where elimination is supposed to occur. Be matter-of-fact and give the child very little attention, such as by smiling, playing games, or singing songs while you are changing his diaper. Instead, give him your attention when he has a BM in the toilet.

  Do not scold or make a fuss while changing the child's diapers. This is attention too and can inadvertently encourage him to soil diapers.

  Be sure to record all accidents on the Daily Progress Record.

- If you see the signals indicating that the child might be going to have a BM at any other time than a scheduled sitting time, take him to the toilet and record the time on the Daily Progress Record. Try to keep the same schedule for one week to develop some predictability for the child and to encourage success. Remember, you have already determined a schedule based upon those times when he is most likely to have a BM.

If you start with bowel training, you can begin urine training once the child consistently has a BM during the first 10-minute sitting time on the toilet, and once he has no more than one BM accident in a typical week.

CHAPTER 9
NEGOTIATING ACCIDENTS
and Related Mishaps
Along the Way

There will inevitably be accidents. Do not blame yourself or think that you are doing something wrong. It is common to feel disappointed and perhaps a bit frustrated or distressed. Try not to let your child know that you are upset. Discuss your feelings with your toileting crew if you want to, and stick to the program even though it is not easy at times.

Accidents

When your child wets or soils his pants, it is very important that you record the accident on the Daily Progress Record. Remember, you are making critical decisions regarding the trip schedule based upon this information, so don't forget to write it down. At the same time, **do not make changes in, or deviate from, the schedule.**

It is essential that you react with very little fuss and attention to accidents. Try to remain calm and matter-of-fact. You do not want to give your child any unnecessary attention for this unwanted behavior. Do not scold, but simply say, "No, you are wet (soiled)," and take the child to the bathroom to change.

 NOTE: Change all wet or soiled diapers in the bathroom because this is the room where toileting is supposed to occur.

Have the child sit on the toilet for about 30 seconds to 1 minute and remind him, "Remember, pee (poop) in the toilet, not in your pants." Do not make him sit longer unless you are reasonably certain he has more to eliminate into the toilet.

Positive Practice

There are varying opinions about the use of positive practice. In my experience, sometimes it is helpful for a child to "practice" where to go potty, and I recommend that most parents at least try it.

1. Once your child has had a toileting mishap, guide him from where he had the accident into the bathroom.
2. Have him pull his pants down.
3. Direct him to sit on the potty for 5 seconds.
4. Have him get off the potty and walk back to where he had the accident and then back into the bathroom again.
5. Sit him again for 5 seconds. Do this five times. He is "practicing" where to go potty. While you are doing this, simply say, "Remember, pee in the potty, not in your pants."

For some children, positive practice can turn into a game. They laugh and get excited. When positive practice turns fun, children may have accidents deliberately in order to begin this entertaining routine with a parent or an adult. **If the child laughs and acts like he really enjoys positive practice, do not continue to use it.**

Other children protest the idea of positive practice and resist going back and forth to the bathroom. If the protests are mild and manageable, continue to practice. If they result in a full-blown meltdown or tantrum, do not continue.

Washing Underwear

When a child begins to urinate in the toilet and to wear underwear, sometimes parents can prompt the child to rinse out wet or soiled underwear in a sink or laundry tub and store them in a container until they can be thoroughly washed.

For older children with the necessary communication and motor skills to comprehend and complete this task, this can be a natural consequence to wetting or soiling.

NOTE: This is not a good choice for children who like to play in the water.

Trouble Initiating Urine Stream

Some children have trouble initiating the urine stream when they are sitting on the toilet. Often this is because they have not discovered that the appropriate place to urinate is in the toilet, not in a diaper or pull-up. These children have been urinating for years in diapers, and now we are asking them to change what they are doing.

They often wait until their toileting time is over and then urinate in the diaper. Other children do not recognize their bodily sensations and the feeling of having to urinate. Yet others have not yet developed control.

Regardless of the reason, here are some activities you can try to initiate urination.

- Slowly pour water over the child's genitals while he is sitting on the toilet. For some children, warm water initiates a stream, and for others it is cool water. If this strategy is successful, always have your child try to urinate first without the water. Continue to use water if he cannot initiate the stream, and over time slowly reduce the amount of water you use until you don't have to use any at all.

- If your child is one who usually urinates while in the bathtub, try placing her hands/and or feet in a plastic tub of water while she is sitting on the toilet and let her play in the water.

For many children who have difficulty initiating urination, once they "get it" and understand that this is what they are supposed to do, they rarely have accidents. So the first time your child urinates in the toilet, be sure that you lavish her with praise and attention as well as her favorite reward. You want her to continue to do it!

Withholding Urine

Five-year-old Jack consistently eliminates in his pants 10-15 minutes after his scheduled sitting time is over. His toileting team is very frustrated, because every time they change the schedule, he changes, too.

Jack does not urinate in the toilet. In fact, he believes that he is supposed to urinate in his diaper and waits until he has a diaper on before urinating. This is quite common, especially for a somewhat older child.

Here again we are asking a child to change what he has been doing for years. Once Jack and other children like him first urinate in the toilet, they usually grasp the new expectation very quickly and rarely have accidents any more. The secret is to succeed in getting the child to urinate in the toilet.

What to Do?

1. Make sure you are following the toileting schedule.

2. Make sure you are using a powerful reward; something the child really likes.

3. About 20-30 minutes before the child's scheduled trip to the toilet, give him extra fluids. Water is best, but diluted juice also works. Give him as much as he will drink.

4. At the scheduled sitting time, sit the child on the toilet for 3 minutes. Be sure to use a timer.

5. Take a 10-minute break. Do not put a diaper or pull-up on the child. Keep him in the bathroom. Give him more to drink and perhaps some salty snacks so he will be thirsty. It is O.K. for him to play in the bathroom. If he starts to urinate, immediately place him on the toilet.

6. After the 10-minute break, sit the child on the toilet again for 3 minutes.

7. Repeat this cycle of 3 minutes on the toilet and 10 minutes off as often as necessary until he urinates in the toilet. Once he urinates, have a party!

If you are going to try this approach, choose a time from the schedule when the child is most likely to uri-nate. Eventually, the child's bladder will become so full that she will not be able to hold it any more, and that's when you want her to be in the bathroom, preferably on the toilet!

 NOTE: It is good to attempt this on a weekend when you have more time and more opportunities to try.

Finally, once they have urinated in the toilet the first time, for some children it is best that they begin to wear underwear, even if it is under a pull-up. By doing this, we are moving them closer to getting rid of pull-ups altogether.

Incomplete Emptying of the Bladder

When some children urinate in the toilet, they do not completely empty their bladder. You may notice this because the child is consistently wet within 30 minutes to 1 hour of having urinated in the toilet.

When this happens, be sure to watch and listen to the child's stream. If the stream is light, or of short duration, ask the child to count slowly to 10 once he has finished urinating. Then ask him to "try again." Usually he will urinate a second time. If he is unable to count to 10, you can do it for him. You can also set a timer for a 10- to 15-second break and then ask him to try once more. If he consistently urinates a second or even a third time, be sure to communicate this to your team so everyone follows through with the procedure.

FAQs

What If My Child Doesn't Care If He Is Wet?

A: It is quite likely that your child does not care if she is wet because being wet is not uncomfortable for her. After all, she is familiar with being wet because she has lived with wet diapers or pull-ups for many years. We have to *teach* her that being dry is the more appropriate behavior. Don't worry, but learn how to do this in Chapter 10.

CHAPTER 10
OTHER BOWEL
TRAINING OBSTACLES
and Predicaments

Learning to have a bowel movement in the toilet can be challenging for some children, especially those who have irregular bowel function, such as loose stools or constipation. Here are some ideas for how to deal with these issues.

Constipation

Constipation means that bowel movements are less frequent and are difficult or painful to pass. It is often caused by a diet that does not include enough fiber. Drinking or eating a lot of dairy products can also cause constipation. The condition can be worsened by repeatedly waiting too long to have a bowel movement.

How to Treat Constipation?

- Make sure your child eats fruits or vegetables at least three times a day. Recommended examples are raisins, apples, plums, prunes, grapes, apricots, peaches, pears, beans, peas, cauliflower, broccoli, and cabbage. Be sure to cut raw fruits and vegetables into very small pieces to prevent choking.

- Increase the amount of fiber in your child's diet. Bran is a high-fiber food that is a natural stool softener. Include bran flakes, bran muffins, shredded wheat, graham crackers, oatmeal, brown rice, whole wheat bread, and high-fiber cookies. For children over 4 years of age, popcorn is a great high-fiber food.

NOTE: The American Academy of Pediatrics (www.aap.org) recommends that children younger than 4 not be fed any round, firm food unless it is cut into small pieces no larger than one-half inch. Children under 4 do not have a full set of teeth and cannot chew as well as older children, so large chunks of food may lodge in the throat and cause choking. This includes popcorn, raw vegetables, and whole grapes.

- Decrease constipating foods in your child's diet. These are generally cheese, yogurt, ice cream, and cow's milk.

- Increase the amount of pure fruit juice that your child drinks. Orange juice will not help constipation as much as other fruit juices. Apple juice is constipating in some children.

- Increase the amount of water your child drinks daily.

- Introduce more exercise, such as walking, running, and jumping.

- If a change in diet does not relieve your child's constipation, give a stool softener every day with breakfast or dinner for one week. Unlike laxatives, stool softeners are not habit forming. They work within 8-12 hours. Milk of Magnesia, Metamucil, Citrucel, and mineral oil are stool softeners that you can buy at your local drugstore without a prescription. Keep mineral oil in the refrigerator so that it will mix easier with juices or applesauce.

- Do not give any suppositories or enemas without consulting with your health care practitioner.

> **NOTE:** This information is intended to inform and educate and is not a replacement for medical evaluation, advice, diagnosis, or treatment by a health care professional.

Digestive problems and stool abnormalities are present in a large number of children with autism spectrum disorders. Many children display problems with enzyme deficiencies, chronic indigestion, gas, and loose stools. These issues should be discussed with and evaluated by your health care provider.

Hiding

> "I always know when Melanie is having a BM because she runs and hides in a corner of her bedroom. She gets awfully quiet, and when she comes out she is all smiles."
>
> – Mother of 4-year-old child with Down syndrome

Hiding – another common occurrence related to toilet training – may be a child's way of obtaining privacy. The goal on these occasions is to have the child "hide" in the appropriate room, the bathroom. Once you've noticed she is hiding, direct her to a corner of the bathroom and leave her alone. When she begins to run into the bathroom to hide on her own, you can start to work on removing her diaper and sitting on the potty.

Withholding Bowel Movements

Some children are afraid to have a bowel movement in the toilet. Perhaps they had a painful bowel movement in the past, or they are afraid of the toilet or "losing" part of themselves. Other children only have a BM in a diaper and scream and tantrum until you give them a diaper to use. All these children withhold bowel movements until circumstances fit their strong preferences, usually a diaper and privacy.

What to Do?
- Provide a relaxed bathroom environment with calming music, toys, and other suitable activities. Keep your voice gentle and soothing.

- Sit the child on the toilet for 10 minutes, take a 20-minute break, and sit him again for 10 minutes. Keep the child in the bathroom during the break and do not put a diaper on him.

- Do not tell your child to "push" when he is trying to urinate or have a BM. This prompt may cause him to withhold. Instead, prompt him to "relax," and then let nature take its course.

- Make sure that the child is physically well supported and has activities he likes to do while sitting.

- Provide information.
  - Some children need factual information. They respond to a poster or life-like drawing of the digestive system with an explanation of each part of the system and the role each plays in the digestion of food. Such posters may be found by searching *digestive system* in Google Images (www.google.com) or looking in an encyclopedia. The purpose of such a discussion is to describe the development of feces as human waste and what is ultimately supposed to happen to this waste. This approach presupposes that the child understands the concepts involved.

  - A detailed story that describes the toileting process helps some children. Such teaching stories simply and clearly describe the steps in the toileting routine as described in Chapter 7: *Final Preparations.*

- Make sure you are using the most powerful reward you can think of. If unsure, go back and review Chapter 4: *Travelers' Compensation: Using Rewards.*

- Check to see that your child is well hydrated. If he is not getting enough liquid, his stools cannot flow properly.

Dealing with bowel issues can be very trying for everyone, and it is easy to give up. **If you are thinking about giving up, consult a health professional.** Most major medical centers have nurse practitioners or others who specialize in the treatment of toileting problems. Someone should be able to design a more aggressive and individualized program that will help you and your child succeed.

Andrew, 12 years old, is legally blind. He has cerebral palsy and a seizure disorder. His present functioning is described at about the 2-year age level. Andrew urinates in the toilet on a schedule, but he has never been successfully bowel trained. He waits until he is home from school; bowel movements occur between 4-5 p.m. When a family member tries to get him to sit on the toilet while he is defecating, Andrew interrupts the bowel movement and waits until he is off the toilet. Then he finishes defecating in his pants.

Andrew's favorite activity is listening to music. His parents decide that music will be his reward for defecating in the toilet. They begin the 10-minute trip to the toilet immediately after school. The 20-minute break occurs in the bathroom, followed by a second 10-minute sit on the toilet. Andrew continues to "wait" until the second trip is finished. After one week, his parents decide to keep with the 10/20 routine until bedtime, if needed.

The second day, Andrew has a BM in the toilet at 6 p.m. Within one month, Andrew is consistently having BM's in the toilet during the first sit and has no further bowel accidents in his pants.

CHAPTER 11
YIELD FOR DRY PANTS
The Ultimate Triumph

It really doesn't matter how often one uses the bathroom, as long as one's pants stay dry in between trips to the toilet. Staying dry is the act that is needed for successful continence. All of us have to learn to "hold" urine and feces until a toileting opportunity arises.

The same applies for our children. We want them to learn to make use of the scheduled toileting opportunities and to stay dry and clean in between.

Eventually, some children learn to recognize their personal feelings of fullness and the need to use the toilet. Others simply learn to use the toilet on a schedule and keep pants dry/clean in between bathroom trips. It is very difficult to predict at early ages in which category your child will fall. Therefore, teach what is expected, and your child will be successful regardless.

Did You Know?
The first step in the toileting developmental sequence is becoming aware that elimination has occurred. The second is that the process of voiding is happening, and the final is recognizing the urge to void before going.

Pants Checks and Dry Pants Rewards

In 1973 Foxx and Azrin first recommended the behavior strategy of pants checks. I find the strategy useful for many children even today, especially those who continue to have accidents and are seemingly unaware that they are wet.

Once your child has begun to urinate in the toilet

and is having, on average, three or fewer accidents a day, implement pants checks and begin to reward periods of staying dry in addition to rewarding elimination in the toilet. Use two rewards, the more powerful reward for staying dry and a lesser reward for eliminating in the toilet. The more powerful reward is used for the most critical outcome, that of ultimately staying dry.

The best time to start pants checks is at the midpoint between sitting times. If the child has scheduled trips to the bathroom at 7:30 a.m. and 10:30 a.m., for example, the best time for pants check is 9 a.m.

Basic Schedule

7:30 a.m.:	Potty trip
9:00 a.m.:	Pants check
10:30 a.m.:	Potty trip

Pants Check Procedure

1. Ask the child, "Are you dry?" If the child is at school or in another public place, take the child into the bathroom. Have the child feel inside his pants. Initially check him yourself, too.

2. Enthusiastically praise him if his pants are dry and give him a powerful reward.

3. Remind him to continue to keep his pants dry and use a picture prompt, if needed, to make your expectation clearer.

4. The child does not sit on the toilet at a pants check unless he is wet or soiled, or it is a scheduled sitting time. Follow the procedure in Chapter 9 for managing accidents if he has had one.

5. Record a D for dry or U for urine in the Pants column of the Daily Progress Record and sit the child at the next scheduled sitting time (10:30 a.m. in this case). Continue pants checks throughout the day at the midpoint between sitting times.

Gradually lengthen the time between pants checks. For example, if the child is consistently dry at the 9:00 a.m. pants check for two weeks and has no accidents between the scheduled trips to the toilet at 7:30 a.m. and 10:30 a.m., increase the interval between pants checks and change the pants check time to 10:30 a.m., the scheduled sitting time.

New Schedule
7:30 a.m.:   Potty trip
10:30 a.m.:   Pants check, then potty trip

---

1. Have the child check his pants right before he sits on the toilet at 10:30 a.m.

2. Praise and reward him when his pants are dry.

3. Remove the reward for urinating in the toilet at 10:30 a.m. and simply praise him when he does so.

4. If he does not urinate in the toilet, remind him to keep his pants dry and record U or D on the Daily Progress Record. Remember, the most desirable accomplishment is dry pants.

5. Check him again at the next scheduled pants check and continue the toileting trips as planned.

6. Once he is consistently dry at the next pants check, change the time of pants check to just before sitting time.

7. Continue to fade rewards for urinating in the toilet while increasing the time between pants checks.

You will likely move to one reward for staying dry all morning, a second reward for staying dry all afternoon, and a third at bedtime. Eventually, the child receives one reward for staying dry all day.

Remember the mom who wanted to use the car wash as a reward? This is where she might choose to use this reward – when her child is dry all day. This whole process will take several weeks. If at any point, accidents start to reoccur, reinstitute more frequent dry pants checks.

> **NOTE:** Continue to modify the child's toileting schedule as appropriate. Some children gradually learn to withhold urine for longer and longer time periods and do not need to sit on a two-hour schedule but can progress to a three- or even a four-hour schedule.

Hearing Judith speak turned a light on for me. I could never understand how Victoria could be dry one day and have a total loss of control the next. Judith related how a child might not know that they were supposed to be dry. We switched the reward for being dry, and our daughter showed immediate progress. We are confident now that we're going to be successful.

— Cindy, mother of a 6-year-old daughter with Phelan-McDermid Syndrome (22q13 Deletion Syndrome)

Our school staff struggled with a first-grade boy who was not fully toilet trained and had some serious emotional issues. Judy's program was instantly successful. Most important, this child does not have to endure embarrassing moments any longer, and he feels successful – a feeling he does not often have. My sincere gratitude.

— Mary Tangora, elementary resource teacher

CHAPTER 12

CREATING INDEPENDENT TRAVELERS

The eventual goal for most children is to be able to travel to and use the toilet without assistance. For many children, even those with special needs, this goal is achievable by using prompt fading and creating self-initiation.

Fading Prompts

In order for your child to master independent toileting, you must eventually begin to fade your prompts and your presence from the bathroom. Stop prompting her once your child knows her toileting routine. Silently wait for her to complete each task and occasionally praise her. When she can complete the routine by herself, leave the bathroom before her at the end of the routine (perhaps while she is drying her hands after washing them). Say something like, "I'll meet you in the kitchen" or "Let me know when you are all done." Smile and praise her again when she is finished.

As the child shows you that she can independently complete each step, begin to leave earlier and earlier in the routine until you are no longer needed and she is able to complete each step of the routine without you.

Creating Self-Initiation

The next task in creating independence is to teach your child to self-initiate the toileting routine. This means your child recognizes the need to go to the bathroom and goes! For some children, this means they recognize a full bladder or feel the pressure of a bowel movement. For others, this means that they simply recognize that toileting is the next scheduled activity and then go.

In either case, we usually want the child to go alone and complete the toileting routine independently (unless this is an unrealistic expectation because of physical limitations or other special needs). That is why you have worked so hard at fading your prompts and your presence, as described above. You don't want to have to ask if your child wiped, flushed, washed hands, etc. You have spent days – maybe weeks – teaching independence, so now we have to work at creating self-initiation and trust that your child can accomplish this, too.

Pair Verbal Prompt with Routine Activity

By now you should have established a rather consistent sitting schedule, and your child should be completely dry for most days of the week. He is able to complete the toileting routine reasonably independently as well. Begin to pair your verbal toileting prompt with a routine activity that usually occurs right before or right after the scheduled sitting time.

Use the same verbal prompt for about 2-3 weeks. You can even use this verbal prompt while you are fading your presence in the bathroom. Examples of prompts include:

- Lunch is finished; it's time to go potty.
- Movie's finished; time to go toilet.
- Bus is coming; time to go potty.
- Bath time, it's time to pee.

Fading Your Presence

If you still need to accompany your child into the bathroom at this point, be sure to start to fade your presence. For example, (a) you walk him to the door but do not go in; (b) you walk him close to the door; (c) you walk to a neighboring room; and finally (d) you stay where you are.

Gradually drop words from the verbal prompt. Because you have been saying exactly the same words for the past several weeks, and your child has gone into the bathroom after you have said them, he will think of the missing words and complete the routine even though you have not said the final word(s) out loud. Wait patiently. If he does not move towards the bathroom, repeat the prompt.

Week 1: "Lunch is finished; it's time to go potty."

Week 3: "Lunch is finished; it's time to."
    (Child thinks, "go potty.")

Week 5: "Lunch is finished; it's time."

Week 7: "Lunch is finished; it's."

Week 9: "Lunch."

Week 11:
- Say nothing after lunch and wait for the child to go into the bathroom.

Because you have established the routine of going to the bathroom after lunch every day, and your child can complete the routine independently, he will automatically go to the bathroom every day after lunch. You will not need to tell him to do it, and he will not need to ask permission. **Yeah!! Independent and successful toileting!**

FAQs

Is It Realistic to Expect the Child to Tell Me When He Has to Go to the Bathroom?

A: Typically developing children who recognize the urge to void and need help generally comprehend spoken language and can use words to express them selves. Therefore, it is quite realistic to expect such children to tell someone when they need to use the bathroom. However, many children with special needs do not recognize the urge to void and, even if they do, they do not grasp easily the concept of asking for help. In addition, many have restricted communication abilities. Some can use and understand simple spoken language, but many are nonverbal. These children might understand and use sign language or gestures, communicate using objects or pictures, or even convey information through their actions and behavior. Therefore, it may be realistic, but it may not be desireable. Read more about this on the following page.

Regardless of how children with special needs communicate, I believe the ultimate goal is independent toileting without help from others (assuming a child has the motor skills to become independent). **We want the child to trav-**

**el to the bathroom, eliminate in the toilet, and complete
the routine by himself.**

We really don't want to teach him to ask permission to
go or to announce to the room that he has to go. We
want him to get into the bathroom and take care of busi-
ness just like everyone else.

How many of you announce to your coworkers that you
are going to the bathroom? How many of us ask our
spouses for permission? **Think about what is "normal"
adult toileting behavior and teach to that end.** For example, it is normal to ask about the location of a restroom if
you do not know where it is. It is normal to excuse yourself from a room when necessary to go to the bathroom.

If you teach your child to tell you she is going to the
bathroom, she will likely continue to tell you as she
grows up, whether you need to know or not, and then
you will spend valuable learning time reteaching more
appropriate social behavior. **Regardless of whether your
child talks or not, it is possible for most children to learn
independent toileting.**

Potty at School

Many teachers expect students to use a bathroom or
hall "pass" when they leave the classroom to go to the
bathroom. Others expect students to place a name card
into a special pocket on the wall or door. Many set aside
time during the day for the entire class to travel to the
bathroom and take turns toileting. Some schools have
bathrooms inside the classroom, and each student uses

it as he or she needs to. In other words, the toileting procedure differs with the particular school environment and varies as the child changes classrooms and grades.

This can be very confusing for some children with special needs, and especially those with autism, who tend to be directed by routine. So when you establish a routine in one classroom setting (e.g., getting a hall pass), and the child has mastered that routine, be sure to teach a new routine next year if the classroom and the routine changes (e.g., the class goes as a group). Just remember to be aware of what you are teaching and make sure that you are teaching what will be most useful as the child ages.

Sample School Toilet Routine

Get hall pass.

Enter stall.

Close door.

Pull pants down.

Pee.

Pull pants up.

Open door.

Wash hands.

Dry hands.

Return to class.

Where's Potty?

Children do need to learn how to request to use a toilet when one is not immediately available. For children with restricted language, a phrase such as "Bathroom, please" might be appropriate.

For children without language, a picture of a bathroom, toilet, or the universal women's/men's restroom sign might be more appropriate because it is widely recognized. Unfortunately, the sign language sign for toilet is not understood by many of us.

Signing "Toilet"

 Forming the right hand into the letter "t" makes the ASL sign for toilet. The palm side faces away from you. Shake your hand from side to side a couple of times. Some people use a twisting movement instead of the shaking motion.

In my opinion, the best environment to teach a child to ask for the location of the bathroom is in public places, or at a friend's or a neighbor's house. At home, children usually know where the bathroom is and should be taught to go there independently. However, if your child cannot travel to the bathroom alone or depends upon someone to assist him in the bathroom, by all means try to teach him to communicate the need to use the toilet.

A common method used to teach children with limited or no verbal communication skills is the Picture Exchange Communication System (PECS). See the reference for Frost and Bondy (1994) in Resources and References for more information on how to do this.

To sum up, **work towards independence to the maximum extent, given your child's abilities.**

CHAPTER 13
LEAVING HOME

Entering the world of public restrooms is a whole new experience for our children. For some of us, the thought of abandoning the safety and cleanliness of our home bathroom to the world of public restrooms can be anxiety provoking. Some of us worry about germs, inappropriate touching, bullying, and other threats that public bathrooms may pose. Nevertheless, we must face our fears and work hard to teach our children about this world so they are safe and free from potential danger – it's all part of making our children independent.

Public Restrooms

The final phase in teaching independence is helping your child to locate and use appropriate public restrooms. If you are the mom and your son
is under 5 years old, it is generally acceptable for
him to go with you into the women's restroom, if
necessary. However, enlist the support of fathers,
grandfathers, uncles, and male friends to introduce your son to the men's restroom whenever
possible. Some public places have family restrooms suitable for everyone.

Scope out and visit the restrooms in shopping malls, restau-
rants, gas stations, or department stores. You can even use
a public restroom at the beginning of the toileting program
while you are recording your child's current elimination
schedule.

You are on a mission to familiarize your child with a variety
of bathrooms and to determine if your child has any sensitivities, such as to the sound an institutional toilet makes when it
flushes or the feel of a blow dryer on his hands. You want to
show your son what a urinal looks like (even if he doesn't use
it yet). You want your daughter to experience waiting in line
(an all too common experience for women, especially). And
you want the child to become familiar with toilet stalls, rows
of sinks, automatic faucets, and automatic flushing.

Some restrooms are unisex (marked by a sign on
the door). Some are individual bathrooms and
you must lock the door. There is a whole new
world out there waiting for you and your child to explore!!

Progression of Public Restroom Trip Schedule

Slowly introduce your child to this new world in the following manner.

Trips 1-3: Point out the signs and where the restrooms are located to your child. Familiarize yourself with the various signs so that you can duplicate them if you need to (Women, Men, Ladies, Gentlemen, Restroom, Girls, Boys, male and female symbols without words). Start to talk about restrooms. Discuss who might be in there and what they will look like.

Trips 4-5: Start to walk in and explore public restrooms; perhaps you wash your hands there. Ask your child to locate the men/ladies room if he is able to do this.

Trips 6-7: Have your child wash his hands in a public restroom and then leave.

Trips 8-9: Carry a portable potty seat with you for small children. Proceed to have the child sit on the seat, get up, wash hands, and leave. Some toilet seats in public restrooms are unsanitary. Carry anti-bacterial wipes with you to clean the seat prior to sitting your child. If your child is older, teach her to wipe off the seat herself.

Trip 10: Begin to expect the child to urinate; use rewards. Follow the routine. Carry a hand towel and wipes when the child is sensitive to the blow dryer or toilet paper. If your child is sensitive to flushing, make flushing the last step in the routine: first wash hands, then flush the toilet, and leave quickly.

The Hidden Curriculum of Public Restrooms

There are many rules in public restrooms that our children with special needs must be taught. Don't assume that your child will automatically know this information, so be sure to review it. First are some general rules, followed by special rules for boys and girls.

Dos and Don'ts of Public Restrooms
- Close and lock the stall door.
- Be sure to flush when you are finished.
- It is not O.K. to look at people through cracks in the door or by looking under the stall door.
- If you accidentally walk in upon someone using the restroom, say "excuse me," quickly leave, and close the door.
- If there is a line, you must wait your turn.
- Do not comment on any smells or noises in the bathroom.
- Do not comment on how people look.
- Do not start a conversation with anyone you do not know.
- Try not to sit on the toilet seat; place toilet paper on the seat if you must sit down.
- Do not use a toilet that has not been flushed. Try to flush it first. If it does not flush, wait to use a different toilet.

Boys

- Leave at least one unoccupied urinal between you and other boys/men if you can.
- Do not ask someone to go with you to the bathroom unless you need help.
- When you stand at a urinal, look straight ahead, do not look to the left or right.
- Do not make eye contact with other boys or men in the bathroom.
- Do not pass anything under the stall walls.

Girls

- It is O.K. to ask a friend to go into the bathroom with you or to go with a group of girlfriends.
- It is O.K. to say, "I'll go with you," when a girlfriend says she is going to the ladies room.
- It is O.K. to give a unfamiliar girl or woman a compliment when you are in the restroom together.
- It is O.K. to pass toilet paper under the stall wall to another girl or woman.

It [toilet training] was a long, hard struggle, but we succeeded. I remember camping in a state forest campground with our porta potty (outhouses were a problem) and our stopwatch!

– Father of a 12-year-old son with autism

CHAPTER 14
POTTY AT NIGHT

Remember in Chapter 2: *Signs and Signals on the Potty Journey,* when I said that children who are usually dry at night are ready for the potty journey during the day? Children accomplish nighttime training at their own pace. Some accomplish it early, and others take a while. If you are concerned about bedwetting, be sure not to tackle this problem until your child is trained during the day. Here are some approaches that you can try.

Bedwetting

1. Do not punish or blame your child for wetting the bed. He cannot help it and is not doing it on purpose.

2. Make sure other family members do not tease the child for wetting the bed.

3. Cut down on fluids after 6 p.m. or at least two hours before bedtime. This may help if your child has a small bladder capacity, meaning that he cannot hold as much urine as other children who do not wet the bed.

4. Establish and stick to a consistent bedtime. If your child usually goes to bed at 8:30 p.m., try to keep the same bedtime on weekends and holidays.

5. Adhere to a consistent bedtime routine. For many children the bedtime routine includes:
   - Eat a light snack
   - Put on pajamas
   - Brush teeth
   - Listen to a story
   - Go potty
   - Wash hands
   - Get into bed
   - Go to sleep

6. Toilet the child immediately before he goes to bed. Make it the very last thing he does before climbing into bed.

7. Put a plastic or protective coating between the sheets and the mattress if your child does not wear pull-ups or diapers.

8. Toilet the child immediately when he wakes up.

9. Keep records of dry and wet nights to see if there is any pattern. If you notice a pattern, try to figure out what is different about those days and nights. Perhaps he has a later bedtime or too much of a favorite drink.

10. Consider waking up the child and toileting her again when you go to bed. Most children fall back to sleep without any difficulty if you choose to do this.

11. If bedwetting persists, consider checking the child every 1-2 hours for several nights to determine when he wets and set an alarm to toilet the child at that time.

12. Consider using a bedwetting alarm if your child is over 8 years old. The alarm senses when your child has begun to wet and sets off a noise or vibration. Some alarms are listed in the Resource and References at the end of the book.

13. Finally, consult your health care professional if bedwetting persists, and your child is over 8 or 9 years old and fully trained during the day.

CHAPTER 15
POTTY JOURNEY STORIES
from Tour Directors
Who Have Been There

We are nearing the end of our journey and our time together. My hope is that you have thoroughly studied all of the information in this guidebook and carefully thought about your own journey to come.

I have chosen a few personal stories from tour directors who have traveled this journey before you. These stories speak to the power of individualizing the journey to suit your personal circumstances. I don't have all the answers.

Take from me and this book the plan that will guide you, but then use your own creativity, persistence, humor, and strength of character to see the journey through to the finish line. The final destination of dry pants is well worth a sometimes adventuresome trip.

After the Phelan McDermid Syndrome Support Group Conference this summer, Judith Coucouvanis' presentation gave me a refreshing attitude and amped up my confidence that Mikayla could be successful at toilet training. I hadn't given up on the idea, but as I am sure you will also feel from time to time, I was feeling drained. I didn't have that extra energy to be on such a huge schedule, even more of one than I was before. Plus, working full time, I was unsure how easy it would be to work this out with day care and school.

But when we got home, we started. Mikayla had been bowel trained for at least a year and a half to two years. I still to this day am not sure why it clicked all of a sudden, but the bowel training happened seemingly overnight. If she is feeling sick or gets diarrhea, once in a while there is an accident, maybe once every four months or less.

When we got home we just sat on the toilet and rewarded her by stickers when she would sit. We also gave her a sticker if she was dry. We bought a simple journal at the store, and next to the date and time, she put her sticker. Of course, the whole family jumped up and down, hooted and hollered, clapped and hugged her for rewards as well. We kept her in panties at home and at day care and just sent a few changes of clothes. We also sent her sticker notebook and stickers with her and kept them with us everywhere we went. We even bought a potty chair and put it in the back of my car, because if she indicated she had to go, we wanted to make sure she had the means of doing so. We would pull over to the nearest parking lot and take the seat out and let her go. At one of our son's baseball games, she was playing about 15 feet from us on the play toys. As I glanced over, I saw that she had pulled her pants down and squatted to go on the field! I couldn't get upset, because she was doing what I asked of her – not having accidents in her brand-new, pretty panties. It was funny.

Once school started, they were right with us with the sticker rewards, and after about two months of stickers, we began to just verbally reward her, or hug and clap, etc. Once in a while she will have an accident if she is laughing really hard or is too intent on playing Legos or cars with her brothers, but again that is few and far between. She now says "I pee" when she has to go potty. Maybe not the most lady-like way, but at this point, I am sooooo proud of her! I credit Judy for my new-found energy and for the ideas and thank her immensely for sharing with us.

– Jodi Rhoden, mother of Mikayla, age 8, who has
  Phelan-McDermid Syndrome

I attended a workshop (Judy) gave about four and a half years ago when my son was 4 years old. My son (did) not have any interest in working on toilet training; he did not even want to step into the bathroom or agree to sit on the toilet. I had to break things down into very small steps, starting with just getting him into the bathroom. I started with getting him to float toys in a sink full of water – this also helped set the stage for getting him to be more cooperative with brushing teeth, washing face, etc. – all of which were difficult for him due to sensory issues related to an autism spectrum disorder.

Persistently and ever so gradually, I added a little bit more to the experience of being in the bathroom, mostly at first just adding 10-30 extra seconds of time being in the room doing something, usually involved with water play, playing games on the rug, listening to music, reading a story, or watching a portable DVD player. Then I got him to sit on the toilet for just 10 seconds at a time, using an electronic timer so that he always knew when the time was up. We slowly added 5-10 seconds at a time. He earned little rewards for cooperating.

Once we reached 3 minutes sitting on the toilet, I never increased it after that. I figured if he didn't go in 3 minutes' time, he probably didn't have to or wasn't going to allow himself to. I upped the ante a little and let him pick a little bit nicer reward if he "practiced" for 3 full minutes. He started having success at school with urinating before he had success at home, probably because other kids at school were doing it and encouraging him. He also had a great teacher who did a very nice job with all of her students in this regard.

When he didn't transfer that behavior to home, we made up new picture schedules that showed that using the toilet is something that kids do at school and home, and at the mall and the movies, and at a friend's house or at the park, or wherever you are when you have to go. I also started visiting school at lunch, which is the time of day he had success at school. Gradually he transferred this to home with regard to urinating, but not with regard to bowel movements. We were at a standstill for several weeks, but I just kept calmly presenting the idea of having a bowel movement every day, and finally one day he told me on his own that he was ready to go poop on the toilet. It was in mid-May on the airplane on the way home from a trip to Disneyworld that we took to celebrate his fifth birthday. (Silly me ... I hadn't thought of promising to let him go on an airplane toilet in a room the size of a gym locker.)

Once he accomplished a bowel movement on that trip, he was fine with it all the time. The next hurdle was that he had become attached to the feel of wearing pull-up training pants. He realized that children that use the toilet all the time don't wear pull-ups any more, but he didn't like the feel of real underwear.

I decided that I had to come up with some reasons to touch real underwear without requiring him to wear it, because the mention of having to wear it caused him great anxiety. I started doing all kinds of things with underwear. We bought lots of "character" underwear (Thomas the Tank Engine, Blues Clues, Bob the Builder, Batman, etc.). We dressed all the teddy bears and stuffed animals in the underwear, I sewed up the legs of a pair of Thomas the Tank Engine underwear and attached two handles to the waistband to convert the underwear into a "tote bag" that he could use to carry his trains around the house in or to hold in the car, I taught him how much fun it is to shoot the underwear at each other across the room by the waistband like a rubber band, and we took pictures of ourselves wearing underwear on our heads like a hat.

Finally, two months after he first started having bowel movements on the toilet, he told me that for my birthday (mid-July) he was going to put on real underwear "just for a little while so I would have a happy birthday present." He put it on and wore it for several hours. I hugged him and thanked him for that special present. He put the pull-ups back on when he went to bed that night, but the next day he told me that he didn't need the pull-ups any more. And he hasn't worn them since!

So I guess the moral of the story is ... patience, patience, patience, steady persistence. Try to keep your sense of fun and humor, use the rewards (small ones reserved only for success with toileting). Up the ante a little if need be – let him tell you what some of his choices might be for a good reward, and try not to let him see you get frustrated or angry about his lack of success. I tried to remember that I should not act any more upset with him telling me he didn't have to go or didn't want to go than I would act if I had offered him a second helping of mashed potatoes and he turned me down. I would just say, "O.K. Let's just practice your sitting on the toilet for today, and maybe you'll be able to go tomorrow or another day."

If all else fails, throw in an airplane ride. He loved how when you flush an airplane toilet, everything washes down the drain with "blue water." We got some of that blue stuff for our toilet at home on the way home from the airport. Every little bit helps.

To this day, doing laundry is even more enjoyable because every time I wash and fold a pair of his briefs, I remember how glad we both were to have accomplished this skill that gives both of us so much more independence. I called him my little Captain Underpants, a name he thought I made up myself at first. Now he knows that there really is a Captain Underpants character in books by Dave Pilkey, which most boys his age find humorous enough to keep their attention all the way to the end of a chapter and then voilá ... soon you have read a whole book ... you gotta learn to work every angle.

– Maureen Carter, parent and advocate for Kenny,
   now age 8 and doing pretty great

Judy's toilet training strategies gave my students the independence and confidence they needed to flourish!! Judy opened the door for them to focus on learning. Judy helped me with numerous behaviors over the years. The most dramatic results were the results from her toilet training strategies.

A profoundly deaf autistic student who had no success with toileting was way over 4 years old. Judy set up a picture symbol schedule for him, and with her instruction we had him toilet trained in less than two weeks.

A cognitively impaired profoundly deaf 4-year-old came to us also not toilet trained. With just a few modifications to the picture symbols, and she also was toilet trained in record time.

Our third and most triumphant success was a little autistic fellow who was so traumatized by toilet training attempts in his previous class that the mere mention of the word "bathroom" would set him off into a full-blown temper tantrum. Once we used our picture symbol schedule, he caught on quickly and was easily trained and ready to move on to other successes.

These are three dramatic successes. Since then, I have had several other less impaired students who have been just as successful with toilet training. Once the light bulb goes off and students know what is expected, they can be successful, and the sky's the limit! Just that little bit of confidence, and self-esteem can let them soar.

– Diane Brenke, teacher of students with autism and related disorders

Conclusion: Notes for the Road

We have come to the end of our journey together. I sincerely hope that your travels will be successful as you begin your personal journey with your child and your crew. You made a choice to buy this guide, and I trust that you will try to stay the course and follow it to the conclusion. I want to leave you with a few checkpoints of those "must dos" on your journey.

✓ Diligently record successes and accidents on the Daily Progress Record.

✓ Stick to the schedule and do not make random changes.

✓ Make planned changes in the schedule based upon the evidence of your data on the Daily Progress Record.

✓ Use praise and rewards for successes.

✓ Use visual tools to help your child understand the expectations and the routine.

✓ Don't forget to add in rewards for dry pants.

✓ Stay positive, keep your sense of humor, and get help from a professional if your journey stalls, and especially if it comes to a halt.

Final Words: Did You Know?

- You'll save about $800 a year when you no longer have to buy disposable diapers?

- You'll regain an extra 3-1/2 hours a week, the time that you used to spend changing diapers?

- You'll aid the environment by not sending dirty disposables to the landfill?

- Your house will smell like potpourri, not poop-pourri? *(Parents* magazine, June 2005)

Good Luck and Best Wishes for a Successful Journey!

RESOURCES AND REFERENCES

Baker, B. L., & Brightman, A. J. (1989). *Steps to independence – A skills training guide for parents and teachers of children with special needs,* second edition. Baltimore: Paul H. Brookes.

Foxx, R. M., & Azrin, N. H. (1973). *Toilet training the retarded: A rapid program for day and nighttime independent toileting.* Champaign, IL: Research Press.

Frost, L., & Bondy, A. (1994). *The Picture Exchange communication system:* Cherry Hill, NJ: Pyramid Educational Consultants Inc.

Hodgdon, L. A. (1995). *Visual strategies for improving communication, Volume 1: Practical supports for school and home.* Troy, MI: QuirkRoberts Publishing.

Savner, J., & Myles, B. S. (2000). *Making visual supports work in the home and community: Strategies for individuals with autism and Asperger Syndrome.* Shawnee Mission, KS: Autism Asperger Publishing Company.

Schum, T. R., Kolb, T. M., McAuliffe, T. L., Simms, M. D., Underhill, R. L., & Lewis, M. (2002). Sequential acquisition of toilet-training skills: A descriptive study of gender and age differences in normal children. *Pediatrics, 109*(3), 48.

Wheeler, M. (2004). *Toilet training for individuals with autism & related disorders: A comprehensive guide for parents & teachers.* Arlington, TX: Future Horizons.

Websites with Helpful Products and Information Related to Toilet Training

Urine Alarms
www.palcolabs.com
www.pottypager.com
www.bedwettingstore.com

Seats and Chairs
www.access-able.org
www.rifton.com

Miscellaneous Products
www.pottytrainingsolutions.com

Training Pants
www.diaperaps.com

Picture Symbols
www.do2learn.com
www.mayer-johnson.com

Fiber Content of Foods
www.nal.usda.gov

Potty Training Products: Toilet-Time Targets
www.WeBehave.com

A Bit of Everything
www.TEACCH.com

Anatomically Correct Dolls: Potty Scotty and Potty Patty
www.pottyscotty.com
www.pottypatty.com
www.pottytrainingconcepts.com

Books for Children About Potty Training

Reading Level: Baby-Preschool

Capucilli, A. S. (2000). *The Potty Book – for Girls* and *The Potty Book – for Boys.* Hauppage, NY: Barron's Educational Series, Inc.

Foote, T. (2001). *My Potty Activity Book +45 Toilet Training Tips: Potty Training Workbook with Parent/ Child Interaction with Coloring and Creative Fun.* Indianapolis, IN: Tracytrends.

Sawyer, P. K. (2006). *Sesame Beginnings: Potty Time!* New York: Random House Books for Young Readers.

van Genechten, G. (2001). *Potty Time.* New York: Simon and Schuster Children's Publishing.

Reading Level: Ages 4-8

Katz, K. (2004). *A Potty for Me!: A Lift-the-Flap Instruction Manual.* New York: Little Simon.

Frankel, A. (2007). *Once Upon a Potty – Boy* and *Once Upon a Potty – Girl.* Richmond Hill, ON, Canada: Firefly Books.

Borgardt, M. (1994). *What Do You Do with a Potty? An Important Pop-Up Book.* New York: Golden Books.

APPENDIX

A: Toilet Training: The Journey

Date: _____

SKILLS	NEVER	SOMETIMES	USUALLY	ALWAYS
Understands potty words				
Stays BM free at night				
Has potty seat available				
Shows interest in using the potty				
Has regular bowel movements				
Flushes the toilet by oneself				
Tells during or after having a BM				
Stays dry for over 2 hours				
Indicates the need to go potty				
Knows how to urinate in the potty				
Sits on potty for 5 minutes				
Washes hands by oneself				
Urinates in potty with help				
Tells during or after urinating				
Pulls pull-up/underwear down by oneself				
Tells before having a BM				
Wears training pants or underwear				
Uses regular toilet without a potty seat				
Stays BM free (clean) during the day				
Tells before having to urinate				
Wipes urine effectively by oneself				
Stays dry during the day				
Wakes up dry overnight				
Enters bathroom and urinates by oneself				
Urinates while standing by himself				
Enters bathroom and has BM by oneself				
Pulls underwear up by oneself				
Wipes BM effectively by oneself				

Modified from Schum et al. (2002). "Sequential Acquisition of Toilet-Training skills: A Descriptive Study of Gender and Age Differences in Normal Children," *Pediatrics*, 109(3), 48-55.

Appendix

B: Daily Progress Record

Scheduled Sitting Times: ☐ ☐ ☐ ☐
☐ ☐ ☐ ☐

	Day 1		Day 2		Day 3		Day 4		Day 5		Day 6		Day 7	
Date														
Time	Pants	Toilet	Pants	Toilet	Pants	Toilet	Pants	Toilet	Pants	Toilet	Pants	Toilet	Pants	Toilet
6:00														
6:30														
7:00														
7:30														
8:00														
8:30														
9:00														
9:30														
10:00														
10:30														
11:00														
11:30														
12:00														
12:30														
1:00														
1:30														
2:00														
2:30														
3:00														
3:30														
4:00														
4:30														
5:00														
5:30														
6:00														
6:30														
7:00														
7:30														
8:00														
8:30														
9:00														

N = No results   D = Dry   U = Urinated
BM = Bowel Movement   U/BM = Urinated and bowel movement

Total U in Pants for week _____ Total BM in Pants for week_____
Total U in Toilet for week _____ Total BM in Toilet for week_____

C: Monthly Progress Record

Progress Record for Month of _____

	Total Week 1	Total Week 2	Total Week 3	Total Week 4	TOTAL Month
Urine Accidents					
Urine in Toilet					
BM Accidents					
BM in Toilet					

Progress Record for Month of _____

	Total Week 1	Total Week 2	Total Week 3	Total Week 4	TOTAL Month
Urine Accidents					
Urine in Toilet					
BM Accidents					
BM in Toilet					

Progress Record for Month of _____

	Total Week 1	Total Week 2	Total Week 3	Total Week 4	TOTAL Month
Urine Accidents					
Urine in Toilet					
BM Accidents					
BM in Toilet					

D: Travel Crew Journal

This journal is for members of the travel crew. Please record your name, the date, and any problems, comments, ideas, or matters that need to be managed or discussed with your tour director.

Date/Name	
Date/Name	
Date/Name	
Date/Name	
Date/Name	
Date/Name	
Date/Name	

E: Toilet Training Countdown
Checklist for a Successful Potty Journey

Two Months Before

- ☐ Review your child's readiness
  - o Remains dry for 1-2 hours
  - o Mental age of 18-24 months
  - o Formed bowel movements
  - o No medical contraindications
- ☐ Complete: *Toilet Training: The Journey* (Appendix A)
- ☐ Start to teach child how to pull pants up and down
- ☐ Start to teach child to wash and dry hands

One Month Before

- ☐ Complete *Traveler's Reward Survey* (Appendix F)
- ☐ Shop for Essential Supplies
  - o Toilet seat
  - o Rewards
    - ▪ _____
    - ▪ _____
    - ▪ _____
    - ▪ _____
  - o Bathroom books, toys
  - o Underwear or training pants
  - o Pull-ups
  - o Loose-fitting clothing
  - o Timer
  - o Footstool
- ☐ Meet with travel crew and review plan
- ☐ Teach child to sit on toilet if needed (Chapter 6)

Three Weeks Before
- ❑ Collect Data using *Daily Progress Record* (Appendix B)
- ❑ Start to explore public restrooms

Two Weeks Before
- ❑ Make reward poster(s)
- ❑ Prepare communication objects/pictures

A Week Before
- ❑ Meet with toileting crew and develop schedule
- ❑ Make copies of *Daily Progress Record* (Appendix B)
- ❑ Make copies of *Potty Crew Journal* (Appendix D)

The Day Before
- ❑ Set up bathroom with essential supplies

During Your Trip
- ❑ Record results on the *Daily Progress Record* (Appendix B)
- ❑ Remain positive
- ❑ Use your guidebook
- ❑ Vary and replenish rewards
- ❑ Meet weekly with toilet crew to review progress
- ❑ Complete *Weekly (Monthly) Progress Record* (Appendices B and C)

F: Traveler's Reward Survey

Child _____

Recorder_____   Date_____

Mark the rewards that you think this child would try hard to earn.

FOOD		
Candy	☐ M&M's	**Soft** ☐ Jello: Flavor_____
	☐ Skittles	☐ Yogurt: Flavor_____
	☐ Jelly Beans	☐ Applesauce
	☐ Peppermint	☐ Pudding: Flavor_____
	☐ Chocolate: Type_____	☐ Cake: Flavor_____
	☐ Candy Kisses	☐ Doughnuts: Type_____
	☐ Lollipops	☐ Frosting: Flavor_____
	☐ Smarties	☐ Cookies: Type_____
	☐ Fruit Chews	☐ _____
	☐ _____	☐ _____
	☐ _____	
	☐ _____	**Crunchy** ☐ Pretzels
	☐ _____	☐ Corn Chips
		☐ Crackers
Cereal	☐ Cheerios	☐ Potato Chips
	☐ Trix	☐ Doritos
	☐ Fruit Loops	☐ Chex Mix
	☐ Chex	☐ Nuts
	☐ _____	☐ Popcorn
	☐ _____	☐ Carmel Corn
		☐ Trail Mix
Fruit	☐ Apples	☐ Granola Bars
	☐ Grapes	
	☐ Bananas	**Drink** ☐ Milk
	☐ Peaches	☐ Chocolate Milk
	☐ Oranges	☐ Lemonade
	☐ Pears	☐ Milkshake: Flavor_____
	☐ Raisins	☐ Juice _____
	☐ _____	☐ Pop: Flavor_____
	☐ _____	☐ Kool-Aid: Flavor_____
		☐ _____
Frozen	☐ Popsicle: Flavor_____	☐ _____
	☐ Ice Cream: Flavor_____	☐ _____

Reward Survey (continued)

SOCIAL			SENSORY		
	☐	Smiles		☐	Rocking
	☐	Praise		☐	Swinging
	☐	Hugs		☐	Dancing
	☐	Kisses		☐	Spinning
	☐	Tickles		☐	Throwing
	☐	Winks		☐	Dropping
	☐	Clap Hands		☐	Twirling
	☐	Rub Noses		☐	Pouring
	☐	Whistling		☐	Playing with Water
	☐	Singing		☐	Turning Water on/off
	☐	Rubbing Back		☐	Fans
	☐	Patting		☐	Smelling Spices
	☐	Hand Shake		☐	Smelling Perfume
	☐	High Five		☐	Smell – Other_____
	☐	Piggy Back Ride		☐	Blowing Bubbles
	☐	Chase		☐	Jumping on Trampoline
	☐	Peek-A-Boo		☐	Playing with Zippers
	☐	Hide and Seek		☐	Playing with Flashlight
	☐	Airplane Ride		☐	Playing with Ribbons/String
	☐	Talk on Telephone		☐	Hand Cream
	☐	_____		☐	Balloons
				☐	Mirrors

ART & CRAFTS			ACTIVITY		
	☐	Making Pictures		☐	TV Show _____
	○	with popcorn		☐	Movie _____
	○	with pasta		☐	Listening to Music
	○	with string		☐	Listening to Story
	○	with sand		☐	Favorite Character _____
	○	other_____		☐	Looking at Photos
	○	other_____		☐	Looking at Books
	☐	Sprinkling Glitter		☐	Playing Computer
	☐	Drawing/Coloring		☐	Playing Electronic Game
	○	crayons		☐	Playing Ball
	○	pencils		☐	Going Outside
	○	markers		☐	Playing with Legos
	○	chalk		☐	Playing with Puzzles
	☐	Cutting		☐	Playing with Play Dough
	☐	Gluing/Pasting		☐	Bike/Wagon Ride
	☐	Painting		☐	Playing with Stickers
	○	Finger Painting		☐	Playing with Stamps
	○	Pudding		☐	Playing with Tops
	○	Whipped Cream		☐	_____
	○	Soap			

G: Sitting Practice Record

Child:_____ Date: _____ Day #: _____ Day of Week:_____

TIME	Pull-Up/Diaper D/U/BM	TOILET D/U/BM	# SEC./ MIN.	COOPERATION (YES) (NO)	REWARD	NOTES

Elimination Code
D = Dry
U = Urine
BM = Bowel movement
U/BM = Urine and bowel movement

Reward
1.
2.
3.
    The child may not receive the reward at any other time.

Cooperation
Y = sat cooperatively
N = crying, screaming, uncooperative

G: Sitting Practice Record (continued)

Procedure (see Chapter 6)

1. Record 6-8 times to "practice sitting" in the time column.

2. When the time arrives, say: "It's time to sit on the potty." Do not ask: "Do you want to sit on the potty?" (Optional: Show/give the child the appropriate picture or object cue or have the child "check schedule.")

3. Show the child the reward poster and remind the child of the reward.

4. Set the timer for the scheduled sitting time.

5. Praise the child, "Good sitting," and give the reward for sitting cooperatively on the toilet.

6. If the child unexpectedly urinates or defecates in the toilet, praise the child and give an extra reward.

7. Add 10 seconds for each new day the child is cooperative for 75% of the previous day's practice sessions.

8. If the child requests the reward at an unscheduled time, say, "First sit on the potty, then ___." Have the child sit on the toilet. Record on the Sitting Record but do not count it as one of the 6 practice sits.

H: Toileting Routine

1. ❑ Enter the bathroom.

2. ❑ Close the door.

3. ❑ Pull down pants.

4. ❑ Sit down on the toilet.

5. ❑ Pee/Poop in the toilet.

6. ❑ Take toilet paper and wipe.

7. ❑ Flush one time.

8. ❑ Pull up pants.

9. ❑ Wash hands.

10. ❑ Dry hands.

11. ❑ Open the door.

Also by Judy Coucouvanis ...

Super Skills: A Social Skills Group Program for Children with Asperger Syndrome, High-Functioning Autism and Related Challenges

This impressive array of social skills activities is specially designed for elementary-aged students with autism spectrum and other social cognitive deficits. Based on a thorough and comprehensive understanding of the unique characteristics of individuals with ASD, Judy Coucouvanis presents 30 group lessons organized under four types of skills necessary for social success: fundamental skills, social initiation skills, getting along with others, and social response skills. Each lesson is highly structured and organized, making it easy for even inexperienced teachers and other group leaders to follow and implement successfully. The lessons, although fluid, follow a specific format that includes multiple practice opportunities, role-plays, supportive skills to prompt and reinforce, as well as suggested activities for extending skill development at home and in the community. A series of practical checklists and other instruments provide a solid foundation for assessing students' social skills levels and subsequent planning. ISBN 1931282676

Judith Coucouvanis; foreword by Brenda Smith Myles

Code 9937   Price: $39.95

Order online at www.asperger.net

APC

Autism Asperger Publishing Company
P.O. Box 23173
Shawnee Mission, Kansas 66283-0173
877-277-8254
www.asperger.net